T0188757

MASTERS AT WORK

ALSO AVAILABLE

BECOMING A SOMMELIER

BECOMING A CURATOR

BECOMING AN ARCHITECT

BECOMING A FASHION DESIGNER

BECOMING A SPORTS AGENT

BECOMING AN INTERIOR DESIGNER

BECOMING A FIREFIGHTER

BECOMING A NURSE

BECOMING A VIDEO GAME DESIGNER

BECOMING A MIDWIFE

BECOMING A TEACHER

MASTERS AT WORK

BECOMING A FILM PRODUCER

BORIS KACHKA

SIMON & SCHUSTER

New York   London   Toronto   Sydney   New Delhi

Simon & Schuster
1230 Avenue of the Americas
New York, NY 10020

Copyright © 2021 by Simon & Schuster, LLC

All rights reserved, including the right to reproduce this book or
portions thereof in any form whatsoever. For information, address
Simon & Schuster Subsidiary Rights Department,
1230 Avenue of the Americas, New York, NY 10020.

First Simon & Schuster hardcover edition April 2021

SIMON & SCHUSTER and colophon are registered trademarks
of Simon & Schuster, LLC.

For information about special discounts for bulk purchases,
please contact Simon & Schuster Special Sales at 1-866-506-1949
or business@simonandschuster.com.

The Simon & Schuster Speakers Bureau can bring authors to your live event. For
more information or to book an event, contact the Simon & Schuster Speakers
Bureau at 1-866-248-3049 or visit our website at www.simonspeakers.com.

Manufactured in the United States of America

3   5   7   9   10   8   6   4   2

Library of Congress Cataloging-in-Publication Data has been applied for.

ISBN 978-1-5011-5943-5
ISBN 978-1-5011-5945-9 (ebook)

FOR JAMIE AND ASHER

CONTENTS

1

WAIT, WHAT DOES A PRODUCER DO?

Like many film producers, Siena Oberman lives in Los Angeles but works and sleeps wherever she is needed. In early December 2019, that was the vicinity of Gravesend, an old Italian neighborhood in South Brooklyn that was the setting for a low-budget movie she spent months building from scratch, a transgressive—albeit cameo-packed—mob drama titled *The Birthday Cake*.

Tackling her fourth film as a lead producer by age twenty-five, Oberman is definitely an outlier, roughly the same age as the assistants answering her hourly calls to the tax attorneys, movie-star agents, and private equity managers she needs to keep her project afloat. This particular project is a precarious one, a low-budget indie feature held aloft through foreign investment, tax credits, well-connected talent, and the tirelessness of Oberman, the wunderkind without whom none of it would have happened.

One blustery day toward the end of the shoot, filming has been going on for a couple of hours by the time Oberman arrives on set—a stolid Italianate house (rented out by the production) on a modest block, distinguishable now by the noisy generator on the winter-brown patch of front lawn. It's almost 11 a.m. Oberman would have arrived earlier, but she was waylaid by a tense phone call closing the remaining financing. Slight, angular, and shockingly calm—considering the freezing temperature, the thousand stressors, and the caffeine coursing through her—she doesn't look like the most powerful person on the production. In fact, she is and she isn't.

There's the talent. Val Kilmer, for example. There's also Paul Sorvino, who's been delayed after driving many hours into the city; even if he makes it later in the afternoon, the order of the shoot will have to be rearranged. There's the writer/producer/actor team who first pitched the project, including rising star Shiloh Fernandez, musician Jimmy Giannopoulos (the film's director), and filmmaker Raul Bermudez (a writer and producer), who called in enough favors to stud the cast with names that Oberman's backers feel comfortable with (from Ashley Benson to Ewan McGregor). There are the international financiers—one whose money seems stuck in South America, or maybe the Isle of Man, without which Oberman can't pay the crew.

These financiers are technically producers too; some have creative input, some only bring money or connections to actors. Money is power, and power will get you a producer credit on a movie. But in order to *produce* a movie in the sense defined in this book, you need to take responsibility. No matter how powerful you are, you need to be in charge. You need to cajole the financiers; fill out the tax-credit forms; remind the first-time feature director to get enough camera angles; scan the past week's footage for continuity because it snowed; procure money for marketing materials; find a cozy spot in the basement for your financiers so they can watch the shoot on monitors without getting in the way.

These are the problems Oberman had *this morning*, before the Wi-Fi conked out, the fire alarm went off, the actors' union delivered an ultimatum, a crew member's temper flared over all the people on his set. When I asked Oberman, toward the end of the day, whether this was the typical way she allocated her time, she said there was no typical way. "For me the priority is: What's the biggest emergency?"

———

IN *STATE AND MAIN*, David Mamet's wicked satire about a Hollywood film production camped out on location in a small town, a director played by William H. Macy is told that the only horse in town is "booked." "Tell the guy, get me the horse!" he says. "I'll give him an associate producer credit." Then he laughs, adding, "I'll give the *horse* an associate producer credit!" A screenwriter who overhears him (played by Philip Seymour Hoffman) asks a young assistant what an associate producer credit is. "It's what you give to your secretary instead of a raise," says the assistant.

It's a funny scene and, for all its cynicism, a window onto what a producer does. It illustrates the kind of horse-trading (sorry) necessary to get a production off the ground, and it touches on a central paradox of the job: "Producer" is a credit everyone seems to want on a film, but because it applies so broadly, few filmgoers have any idea what a producer actually does.

"Most people outside of the movies just truly don't understand what it means and make the assumption that it's very finance-driven," says one producer. "Which is pretty much not the case. There is a perversion of what the word means that also includes people who finance—which is a version of buying the credit without doing the work." Or as Lynda Obst, a producer and the author of the industry memoir *Hello, He Lied*, told me, "It's the only title anyone can just decide to join. But some of us have to stay and make the movie."

There's an old Hollywood joke: How many producers does it take to screw in a light bulb? Twelve: one to screw in the light bulb, eleven to take credit for it. Those eleven people may be movie stars taking a credit in exchange for a pay cut; family members cut in on a deal; celebrities lending their imprimatur; or, far more often, financial partners who have helped pay for and sell the movie but done little else.

This isn't a book about the eleven who take credit; this is about the so-called creative producer, the one who does the work. If only it were as simple as screwing in a light bulb. The best way to figure out what it entails is to watch someone do it. Over the summer and fall of 2019, I followed three exceptional producers at different phases of their careers, watching how their jobs evolve hour to hour and day to day. In following all three and interviewing a wider array of people in Hollywood and independent film, I got a sense of how the job progresses from decade to decade of a producer's life—and then, even more broadly, how the industry has changed over those decades, from the heyday of the studios to the reign of the streaming platforms.

Oberman, the twentysomething in charge of *The Birthday Cake*, isn't exactly a typical up-and-comer, but she occupies the niches of a producer just making her bones. She works mostly on movies that cost less than $5 million and takes in fees in the five figures. She barely has time to sleep and, having fewer people to delegate to, must wear many more hats.

Higher up the chain is Fred Berger. Now thirty-nine, he's one of two partners in Automatik, a young production company that's pushing up into budgets as high as $100 million on films and TV streamers. Berger had his first big break as one of the lead producers on the prestige blockbuster *La La Land*, and since then he's rapidly built up credits and experience. He's a talented and confident negotiator with deep artistic bones, adept at handling bigger projects and egos, but still working his way up to permanent stability.

Finally, I spent time with Michael London, who at sixty-one has been through several transformations in the industry and his own career. He's been an executive at a mainstream production company as well as a studio (Fox);

a semi-independent studio-backed producer; a completely free agent riding the early-aughts indie boom to bring the world *Thirteen* and *Sideways*; and the head of a private equity–backed finance and production company. Now he's independent again and doing far more TV than he ever imagined doing.

These three producers have a lot in common (they work on the more artistic "indie" side of the street—none have made a Marvel movie), but they're also as different as any three people separated by age, temperament, and background. There's a consistency in what they do and the traits that make them effective. They are strategically calm and very good at getting what they want, having mastered the art of figuring out what other people need. They can tell when a negotiator is serious and not just blowing smoke, but they also have the spark of defiant optimism it takes to convince themselves and others a long shot is worth taking (all movies start out as long shots). What they do isn't easy, but it's never dull. It's a high-stakes emotional roller coaster whose ultimate goal is showing people a good time.

You're probably still asking: What do they *do*? Explaining that requires breaking down the process of how a movie gets made. Like many businesses, it used to be both simpler and less interesting. In the days of the studio system, Warner Bros. or Paramount Pictures did everything. It had actors with seven-year contracts, in-house marketing teams and directors, and its own house producers based near the lot. A producer worked for Paramount, for example, and was responsible for developing the script, assembling the cast, shepherding a project through filming, and handling the marketing and release. These producers were either high-powered executives or their more hands-on minions, but in either case they were company men (and a few women). They did the management for the studio—the giant factory whose many workers banded together to bring films to fruition.

As studios became less monolithic, a more outsourced system developed. Producers were still in charge of finding and developing projects, but they became more independent. In the '70s some directors set themselves up as production companies. As the actors gained more clout in the '80s and '90s they, too, set up production companies. One of the best teams of producers works at Plan B Entertainment, Brad Pitt's production office. The studios, meanwhile, became acquirers and resource providers, in some cases literally providing soundstages and in others acquiring already-made movies. A company that doesn't make movies at all but only acquires is a distributor; all the studios, TV networks, and streaming platforms buy material, but only some also help make it. (Networks and streamers often partner with studios, though many have studio arms of their own.)

Nowadays, a movie that starts with a producer can take one of two tracks. If the producer has a "first-look" deal with a studio or platform, she gets office overhead covered by the studio in return for taking any project she packages (gathering up talent, revising the script, roughing out the budget) to that studio first. If the studio refuses, she can take it elsewhere. If the producer manages to get any studio behind an unfilmed project, the deal is done; the producer gets her 5 percent of the budget (or some agreed flat fee) and becomes the hands-on manager of a company-owned film in progress.

The other route—independent filmmaking—is more complicated. This is the route that tends to generate those extra producer credits. A sample roster of producers is effectively an anatomy of how an independent movie got made: two managers of big-name actors who took a pay cut; the person who introduced the screenwriter to the director; a line producer who worked overtime to get a tax credit; two indie producers who managed the project; the author of the originating book; and maybe a horse wrangler for good measure. But the largest number of "producers" on a complicated project consists of financiers who floated the project so it could get made before a studio laid a hand on it.

In order to make an independent movie, the producer must cobble together financiers to pay up-front costs. These are investors, not benefactors. Their money is securely backed by the promise of foreign sales and bridge loans—sometimes even guaranteed by the sales arms of agencies that handle the distribution sales. Then, Lord willing, the movie gets made. In the event of a sale to a distributor, often at a film festival—sometimes in an auction after a major premiere at Sundance or Cannes—the investors get paid back first. They get paid again (as much as 20 percent) if the box office exceeds the budget. The producer is among the last to see that "back-end" money.

One way to figure out who a "creative producer" is on a project is to figure out which person or company *doesn't* put in their own money. All they have is skill and connections;

they don't buy the light bulb, but they screw it in, day by day, and eventually make a good living from it.

Whatever path a film takes, the creative producer is the person who looks out for the project from start to finish. The studio might handle marketing, but it only has so much bandwidth to focus on each project; the producer is the one who makes sure her specific movie gets the care and push it deserves. The director (always) thinks he knows best, but the producer tells him when he's letting the perfect be the enemy of the good.

There's an even easier way for a casual filmgoer to know who the real producer is. In 2012, after years of pushing back against credit creep, the Producers Guild of America instituted a "Producer's Mark," a simple "PGA" beside the names of a small handful of producers who have been able to certify that they fully managed the project. (In the end credits, look for, e.g., "Siena Oberman (pga).")

Even with that settled, it's still difficult to define the job's parameters, because there's no real professional certification behind it, no concrete set of skills or qualifying exam. It isn't oriented toward a task but toward a project, which cannot exist—much less succeed—without the accomplishment of many smaller tasks (some of which, in larger production companies, become jobs of their own). You can think of it as not one job but a succession of them, or an overlapping web. Below is the most elemental rundown:

SCOUT

Lynda Obst will never forget what Peter Guber, whose movies include *Rain Man* and *Gorillas in the Mist*, once said to her: "'A producer is a dog with a script in its mouth.'" Obst continues, "So how you become a good producer, that's a different issue. But you can call yourself a producer if you have a script you can sell."

Fred Berger was a young up-and-comer casting about for projects when he teamed up with producer Jordan Horowitz and Damien Chazelle, a young director with a crazy idea for a jazz dance musical doubling as a love letter to Los Angeles. Michael London was a not entirely satisfied junior Fox studio executive until he went independent, and eventually heard from a friend, Rex Pickett, who was working on a book he originally called *Two Guys on Wine*. Berger and London would probably have been successful without *La La Land* or *Sideways*, but they started out the way so many successful producers do—as dogs with good scripts in their mouths.

Once you've scouted the script, you'll know whom to recruit to help get it made, because if you're a good scout, you've also spotted talented actors, directors, rewriters, and cinematographers as a result of voracious movie-watching and connection-making, either at film festivals or your local theater. And you'll know their agents, too.

DEVELOPER

This is where the canine analogy breaks down: No good producer is merely a retriever. A producer has probably read more scripts, and almost certainly gotten more made, than the screenwriter they're working with. "Development" is another one of those words that sounds baffling to people outside the industry. It's editing and gathering, making a project viable and strong. It's easy to mock studios and producers for giving "notes"—meddling creatively, the cliché goes, to water down a story forged from the pure genius of the creator. In fact, notes can save a project before it even gets off the ground.

Scripts may fail to sell for many reasons, but none of them can get a green light without being coherent, well-defined, and written with an understanding of the practicalities of making the movie. A script needs a clear arc, plausible characters, a plot without holes, and a visual language that conveys information efficiently and elegantly. It needs to connect with an audience emotionally, of course—and a good scout wouldn't champion one that didn't. But practical elements must be conceived with the reality of filmmaking in mind. If a producer knows that no one in Hollywood would pay more than $20 million for a quirky sci-fi comedy, she'll know that sixteen helicopter scenes and a CGI spaceship are just not going to work.

EDITOR

This is the flip side of development; once a movie has been shot, the producer makes sure that the director and editor's cut of the movie or show has a viable path toward success with an audience. So the producer becomes, once again, the overseer. They will offer notes toward meeting certain audience expectations (genre elements, or an Oscar-worthy monologue). They will also hold test screenings with an eye to audience responses, and then deliver the news to the director about what gets high praise and what bored the focus group to tears. Most producers have "final cut" on a project, meaning the ultimate say over what ends up in the movie, but this tends to be a last resort. On TV shows the lead producer, or showrunner, is often the head writer and the lead editor in postproduction, while leaving the shooting to episode directors. The producer as defined here is different. On a film, he has less artistic input but more practical savvy, control, and, ultimately, responsibility.

NETWORKER

Building up a circle of trusted friends and acquaintances is important in most professions, but absolutely essential to producing. Producers connect directors to writers, actors to scripts, and financiers to people who can vouch for their honesty. "I spent five years going to every film festival and networking event I could," says Oberman—beginning when she was still in film school at the University of Southern California. "I realized that if you can bring an actor or money or a big director, if you could make certain connections, then you could get involved in projects by bringing value to them. That's just the quickest way to get into producing."

This is why many producers think it's important to get an early start in the business, while you're young and social. This is why an assistant job at a talent agency, while often grueling or even exploitative, is considered a path toward producing. Fielding calls from people across the industry—and learning, for your boss's benefit, who's important and what they can do—will pay off five or ten years later when you're looking for a green light at Disney or a referral to a cinematographer.

Almost as important as knowing people is knowing things. Even the most casual catch-ups can become pretexts for the exchange of information. You have to find out which actors are unavailable for a role, which writers have exclusive deals at which studios, and which junior agents can get their bosses on the line immediately. Sometimes that knowledge serves a specific project you're putting together, sometimes not. Information arrives strategically or serendipitously, but it's often exchanged during social occasions or unrelated meetings. Information is power in Hollywood, and its exchange depends on a vast network of connections.

SALESPERSON

This function of the job covers more or less every stage of production. When a screenwriter or showrunner makes a pitch to executives or funders, the producer is always there—sometimes physically or on the phone, but also as a coach every step of the way. The producer knows which comparisons to make with other (successful) movies and which to soft-pedal or avoid (the bombs, of course). She knows how much information is enough and what's too much, who would make the perfect director, or just the right name to toss off in order to put the funder at ease.

To get financiers on board, the independent producer will need to secure guarantees or down payments from foreign-film distributors interested in eventually buying the movie for their territories. This is what's really happening at all those swanky film festivals that are ostensibly about premiering movies and building Oscar buzz. "Cannes, Berlin, and Toronto are not just film festivals—they're markets," says Berger, who along with his Automatik partner, Brian Kavanaugh-Jones, had three buzzy films on the festival circuit in 2020. "Most of these projects are introduced at script stage, with director and cast—we hope to get them made, but the independent model depends on proving foreign sales estimates with concrete pre-sales." Producers make the rounds of parties and ski chalets not only to have a good time but to sell their wares. Picture a bazaar with gorgeous views and open bars.

On the other end of a project, there's marketing, which studios may handle—or rather outsource to companies that design trailers, billboards, and Oscar campaigns—but producers must ultimately push to its fullest potential. A good producer knows when a movie trailer isn't working, or where certain billboards need to be, what festivals to submit to in order to ensure the best sale to a distributor, and ultimately what segments of the movie audience are most open to what the filmmaker has done. He also knows how to set reasonable expectations and make decisions accordingly. Perhaps a film has a better shot premiering at the Sundance Film Festival rather than Cannes. Perhaps a prestige picture's buzz depends on a strong per-theater box-office number—meaning it should only premiere in a handful of theaters. Maybe it's worth hitting up an investor for extra cash to keep a star happy, so she'll be more enthusiastic at press junkets. From pitching studios to solving on-set conflicts all the way to strategizing the right release schedule, it's all salesmanship in the end.

DEALMAKER

This skill is related to selling, but distinct. "Closing" deals, whether to secure an actor or a movie's foreign-rights sales, requires paying very close attention to what's in a contract and ensuring there won't be any surprises down the line. Failing to close loopholes can result in disaster—as it did two years ago for Alexander Payne, the *Sideways* filmmaker who was just about to start filming a feature about a Norwegian writer on an American road trip. At the last minute, the writer himself, acclaimed author Karl Ove Knausgaard, changed his mind and pulled out of the project. When other producers heard about it, they blamed it not on Knausgaard or Payne but the producers, or someone who worked for them. "There'll be people fired over that," said one, "and they'll never make another movie without a chain of title," or full ownership of the project.

But dealmaking isn't just closing a contract. As one talent manager said to me, "Deal negotiation is the easiest part of the producer's job. Any dude can negotiate selling Porsches in the Valley." No deal is complete until there's a legal contract, but to get to that contract, many informal agreements must be made. An author may not normally have the power to pull out at the last minute, but an actor "attached" to a project normally does. Sometimes he doesn't sign a contract until the morning of filming starts. Every "deal" up until that point is a matter of commitment, trust, and constant maintenance.

The road to a successful movie is paved with such small agreements, daily feints, and compromises that maximize a film's potential without bruising egos. Berger recalls a recent meeting with a distributor ahead of a smaller film's release—a movie he already knew "was not destined to be a huge hit." He believed it needed a release date that didn't compete with bigger films, and the distributor's three potential dates felt problematic. He could have pressed the point in the blustery manner of the clichéd bloviating producer. Instead, he offered to pull back on publicity and travel expenses that the distributor had agreed to pay for.

"I'm not looking to extract a pound of flesh," Berger says. "I want to make it even more favorable for them and we'll work together for the best outcome for the film." Within ten minutes, a fourth release date had magically opened up. Thanks to a calm approach and preparation, everyone got something. "We both had different agendas walking into that meeting and I was able to get them on board, but not without buy-in. That happens on a daily basis. It's crucial to treat studios and financiers as partners. I win if they win. Most importantly, the film wins."

MANAGER

As the cast and crew sign on and a movie or show moves closer to the shoot, the creative producer's duties transition to hands-on management. It's the part of the job that distinguishes producers temperamentally from other operators in the business. Anne Lai, who spent years nurturing talent through the Sundance Institute's Producing Labs, says that "if there are common themes" among people who gravitate toward producing, "it's like, 'I was the person who put parties together. Or when the kids on the block played kickball, I would organize that.' It's someone who knows how to build teams." A lot of the work toward a smooth film shoot is done in what's called "prep," short for preproduction. The team is finalized, including the people most directly in charge of the crew: the line producer, who oversees day-to-day expenses; the assistant director, who fine-tunes the schedule; and the director of photography (or cinematographer), who handles the individual shots.

Any manager has to balance delegation with direct involvement, and each producer does it differently. Oberman, a young producer on small-budget films that are always logistically touch-and-go, is on set 100 percent of the time. On a shoot of the HBO show *The Leftovers*, whose third season was shot in Australia, the team of lead producers made a few trips during three months of filming and were all there for the weeklong shoot on the final episode.

Whether on set or not, one truth always holds: the better planned the production is, the less the producer has to do. In *Hello, He Lied*, Lynda Obst lists the "Biggest Issues on an Easy (Well-Run) Show," including "where to live," "where to hold the wrap party," and "what to wear." A few pages later comes a parallel list of concerns on a hard show, including "Can we make the day?" (meaning get all the scheduled shots), "Will this movie ever wrap?" and "Will the plug be pulled?"

Management is where you can separate the true creative producer from the hangers-on. Any old horse wrangler can make a connection, and Hollywood is full of skilled deal-makers and information brokers, but only a producer can make a tricky film succeed by balancing all the competing pressures in the service of the film itself. Only the producer can reassure the star she'll get the proper catering and time off, insulate the director from the penny-pinching of studio execs, talk the union out of pulling the plug on a production over a delayed payment.

"It's the only job where you hire your boss," Obst tells me, meaning the director. "And then you continue to be responsible to the studio." Universal or Netflix may be paying the bills, but the producer is managing the production. In a sense she is managing both the boss who makes the project (the director) and the boss who pays for it (the studio)—and mediating between the two. "So the studio can always be incredibly nice to the director, while you interpret what they want to him in a more pleasing way," says Obst. And it's not just about mediating between the financier and the artist; it's about being the only one who can speak up for the project itself.

Jordan Horowitz, Berger's coproducer on *La La Land*, has recently devoted himself fully to independent production after trying a new tactic while prepping for industry meetings. "I remember making a chart of what everybody's priorities were," he says. "Actor, executive, whoever." He was trying to figure out how to meet negotiators where they were—"to see how my priority could intersect with everyone's priority . . . And it was so interesting to see that for the producer, it was the project. The project was never anyone else's first priority."

NOT ALL PRODUCERS DO all of these things all the time or equally well. Those eleven other producers have *some* hand in screwing in the light bulb. Some of them may even be creative producers taking a lighter role on a particular project—either because they don't have the experience to lead a production or because this particular film is a side project helmed by an associate or friend. Oberman, for example, plans to find junior partners to take the reins of a movie with a $300,000 budget so that she can focus on leading bigger-budget films.

She'd consider taking an executive producer credit on that film. Executive producers, or EPs, aren't always financiers. Sometimes they are literally executives—senior office workers at production companies. Other easy-to-confuse roles include associate producers, generally not horse handlers but junior producers assisting the boss. Often, members of a production team will switch off these roles, taking turns as lead producers. And of course, some producers only make deals; some only raise money; some only have creative input; some are really talent managers.

These byzantine arrangements can be learned and navigated with experience, but they make the whole profession seem deliberately opaque from the outside. Most professions, hard as they are to master, at least provide clear career tracks and responsibilities along the way. So what kind of person gets into producing in the first place? Do you have to have been raised in Hollywood—schooled in its hidden hierarchies, unwritten rules, and precise skill sets? Some producers are raised in Hollywood, born to industry connections. But many more are not—could never have dreamed of winding up where they are.

For lots of them, it begins with an obsession, not unlike the bug that afflicts directors or screenwriters or actors—a love of the screen, big or small, that takes years to coalesce into an understanding of how it really works and what their place in it might be. David Permut, whom these days you might call an old-school producer (*Face/Off*, *Hacksaw Ridge*), started out by selling star maps as a teenager in the '60s. He had a subscription to *Variety* in the seventh grade. He wrote letters to directors begging for assistant jobs until he broke through. In his Beverly Hills office, he showed me a reply he received from Frank Capra when he was eighteen.

Fred Berger never went quite that far—but he thought about it. "When I was a kid, I always imagined writing Spielberg a letter pleading for him to let me bring him coffee and donuts on set, even for a day, for the thrill of watching a movie come to life. The fact that I get to walk onto sets—without having to sneak in—is still surreal. I don't think I'll ever lose the feeling that I'm an intruder, getting away with something."

Like many would-be directors, Oberman started making short films in high school with a flip camcorder—"super-low production quality," she's sure to tell me now. She went on doing it through college and film school, even as she realized producing was her real forte.

The producer can be an artist, in a way, but generally is both more and less than one. In most of the stories producers tell about their origins there comes a point where the artistic impulse melds with a practical mindset—a desire to move from conceiving a project to organizing it, making it happen for themselves and others. These are people whose right and left brains are well-connected and equally essential. The organizers of those childhood parties and kickball games now begin helping their film-school friends turn their pipe dreams into projects.

A number of producers interviewed for this book were heavily involved in school drama clubs. Low-tech, communal, and fun, theater might have been the most accessible route toward practicing the art of putting on a show. But as they grew up, went to college, and looked around at their options, theater often felt too limiting.

"I went to school for acting," says Jordan Horowitz. "And right after college I started producing plays with my friends. There was nobody putting the writers and directors and the actors I knew together to do the work that people wanted to do, so I started producing them. I produced some photo shoots, worked at a restaurant, did a bunch of random things, and eventually decided that the New York theater scene was not something I could keep doing, so I started working in the New York film scene."

Sarah Freedman, who in 2019 was an assistant at Michael London's production company, Groundswell, grew up in New York, the daughter of a lawyer and a prominent journalist. "My father used to cover theater, and so we would always see musicals and plays, and I took acting classes," she told me. "My number one love is theater. I was a drama major in college, and I did this program at the Eugene O'Neill Theatre, and I realized it was very insular. Theater didn't need another educated Jewish white girl, but movies could be where my voice might be needed. And I wanted to make more money, but also have a bigger impact, and I couldn't have that with theater."

Freedman was mainly talking about pressing for more diversity and attention to sexism. Her ambitions are fairly common among former drama club kids. Film is a bigger world than theater in size and influence. It's also a place where an organizer of other people's dreams can, eventually, make a good living. For producers, as for many people who work in TV or film, the ambitions toward making money and having a cultural impact go hand in hand. But ultimately, given the time and pain involved, the latter impulse has to be the prime motivator. Because for those with talent and opportunity, there are far easier ways to get rich.

A producer's earliest training, whether as an assistant or in film school or in the mad scramble to get a friend's movie made, generally nets minimum wage at best. A small movie can earn a producer $30,000 if she's lucky, for six months of work. When a production's budget needs tightening, a producer's fee tends to be the first to go—because the boss can't quit.

Ultimately, producers can and often do make *a lot* of money, but they work a lot harder for it than most people in the industry. The money only kicks in after all the work of development, fundraising, talent scouting, and preproduction staffing has been done. If a studio has acquired it by then, the money starts to flow when filming begins—and that 5 percent of the budget can mean millions. That said, larger projects are often handled by production companies rather than individual producers, with fees feeding into the entire firm's revenue. Some eventual percentage of net profit is often worked into the deal, but as producers are among the last to be paid, it takes the rare blockbuster for the eye-popping money to kick in.

For young aspiring producers, many of them assistants, that is a long way out. As in so many cultural professions, low pay at the lowest rungs results in a structural bias toward children of the upper middle class; indeed, the only producers I talked to from less advantaged backgrounds had worked their way through a lab program or accrued savings in finance or marketing.

In other words, the path of the producer is generally taken by those who have other options. In the old days of the European refugee studio moguls, the profession was a launching pad for working-class strivers. Today it draws people who might otherwise have gotten advanced professional degrees or gone into business. "It was a generation of college dropouts, it was much more Wild West out here," says Berger of the midcentury heyday of MGM and the rest. "But it's become a 'cool' career for the Ivy League now, and it's hypereducated, not necessarily to the benefit" of the profession.

Berger went to the University of Pennsylvania, majoring in Philosophy, Politics, and Economics (PPE). He thought about law school, and his first-generation-immigrant parents encouraged that path. "From Penn, a lot of kids go into banking and law," he says. Instead, after graduation, he took an unpaid internship at Focus Features. "Everyone I knew was earning big salaries out of school. I got $7 a day for lunch, three days a week, waiting tables on off days. Still working for my dad on weekends, still living with my mom, still commuting to the city . . . and I was having a blast, because I was one small step closer to the film world."

Interning is one way to break through, but a slow one. Film school is an obvious first step for many, with the University of Southern California being the gold standard. It's also a storied networking school, though it bears remembering that Steven Spielberg was rejected by USC, went to California State in Long Beach instead, and did just fine. It may or may not teach you the skills you need, but film school is a natural hub for the brightest and most passionate budding filmmakers.

Film programs, whether undergraduate or MFA, definitely have their detractors. "There are of course exceptions, but I'm not a huge advocate of film school for aspiring producers," says Berger. "I was dissuaded from pursuing it by my industry mentors, and it turned out to be wise advice. Unlike law or medicine, this is a job best learned by doing. If you already know you want to make movies, that's an edge—dive right in."

Without question, film school provides social opportunities. Oberman was already meeting future financiers back then, and one of her classmates wound up becoming an executive in her production company. There are worse ways to break into a field, whatever niche you end up occupying, than finding an affinity group in your early years, absorbing the arcane mores and secret passwords, and facing the world with them together.

Just don't expect to come out knowing anything firmly applicable to the way things actually work. Hollywood is a knowledge economy, and production is a craft. Whether you go to film school or not, you have to do it—or at least some parts of it—to know how. You have to make mistakes, defer to bosses who seem to have it easy, toil as an assistant with little more than a futon to your name. The early years of an industry career are a crucible, fun and frustrating and formative. If you can survive them with your drive and passion intact, you've got a shot.

2

THE APPRENTICES

Odds are that if you've recently graduated from film school, you aren't quite sure what to do next. Most producers aren't set on their path at age twenty-two. But let's reverse-engineer the question. What have producers done to put themselves on the path?

In a certified trade like plumbing, apprenticeship is a long-established phase of the job. But professions have them, too (clerking for a judge, serving as a medical intern). Hollywood is dominated by guilds, which evolved among tradesmen in the Middle Ages in part to formalize apprenticeship. That structure survives today in a very different setting, the TV and film industry, a business that runs on assistants. Arriving in droves after graduation every year, those assistants are the future producers, executives, and agents of the next generation.

Most common among these jobs is a lowly position in one

of the mega-agencies that dominate Hollywood: the United Talent Agency, Creative Artists Agency, International Creative Management, and William Morris Endeavor—better known as UTA, CAA, ICM, and WME. Each has hundreds of talent agents with thousands of clients—clients that include not just actors and directors but screenwriters, brands, and producers. In recent years, some have grown large enough to open branches that broker foreign film sales, offer development money, and even package movies (in essence becoming producers).

"They call it boot camp or grad school," says Sarah Freedman, whose assistant position at WME was her first job after moving out West. Her mentor at a production company where she interned in New York took her out to lunch and said, "You've got to work at an agency." Instead, she landed at the reception desk of the Weinstein Company—until its head, Harvey Weinstein, imploded under many, many sexual-assault allegations. Seeing few options in New York, Freedman decided it was time to move to Los Angeles.

Once in L.A., she explored agencies in earnest. "I cold-called a bunch of places. I did LinkedIn sleuthing and had an IMDbPro trial account"—the Internet Movie Database has a premium portal with industry contacts—"and I was sending emails all the time. I would call UTA and be like, 'Oh, I'm so sorry, I came in for an interview and I can't remember the HR person's name. Do you have their email?'" When she reached an HR person at WME, they asked if she could come in right away.

Like most assistants, Freedman spent her days answering calls, keeping her boss's schedule, reminding her what needed to be done ASAP. She made tight-knit friends, and now they're growing up together in Hollywood, tipping each other off to opportunities and sharing intel on bad bosses to avoid, vouching for each other as they begin their slow ascent up the ladder. "The other assistants were by far the best part, they're why I have friends, and support."

Berger sometimes laments that he didn't start in the agency mailroom. "I'm lucky I was able to bypass the trial by fire, but it also has its real benefits," he says. "Like college, you enter alone, but graduate with a 'class' of peers that become lifelong friends and collaborators." He often advises interns to start at agencies post-college; when he sees them six months into their agency experience, "They have a dramatically different understanding of the business.

They don't even realize how much they're absorbing by osmosis—it's night and day."

Agencies are factories of information. Junior agents are assigned to "cover" specific studios and networks, meeting with executives and learning about every project in development. Senior agents are only good at their jobs if they know about every project in every desk drawer in L.A. County. It's the only way they can make sure their clients have access to exactly the right work at the right time.

Assistants have to quickly learn the hierarchy that governs which callers to stall and which to put directly through to their bosses. They're the ones who maintain the call sheet—the rolling list of calls to make and return. In order to stay apprised of their bosses' projects, they also listen in on almost every single call.

"You gain an instant network," says Berger. "You'll quickly find out whether representation appeals to you. If not, you'll be listening to calls with every corner of the industry—producers, execs, writers, directors, etc.—and at some point, you'll probably say, 'Oh, I want to do what that person does.' Either way, most jobs require a year or two on an agency desk, so it's a useful on-ramp. It's worth it, but it can be a tough year."

Freedman would agree with that. "It's such a hub of gossip and information," she says, "but it's about how do you cut away the toxicity?"

Two years ago, Hollywood assistants began organizing, aiming to join one of the industry's unions, based on what had long been common knowledge: the lives of many assistants are hell. Under the hashtag #PayUpHollywood, a group of writers ran an online survey of assistants. They found that salaries had been stagnant (even accounting for inflation) for a generation (around $15 an hour), and that out of 1,500 respondents, 100 reported having had an angry agent throw something at them. It's one thing to hear stories about a monster like Harvey Weinstein hurling insults and staplers, another to see evidence that it's an accepted practice. Those rates have since gone up in reaction to the movement, to over $20 an hour in most firms.

Freedman won't get into details of what she says was a rough experience at WME, except to refer me to published stories about assistants. She got to her desk at 7:30 a.m. and left at 8 p.m. every day and never did much more than administrative work. "To put it in the nicest way," she says, "I did not see myself being an agent." After a little more than a year at WME, she'd had enough. "I wanted to do something where I get to do development, be creative." When she found out Michael London was looking for an assistant, she jumped on it. When we met, she had been his assistant for several months.

Another junior employee at Groundswell is Jordan Mahoney, who was an assistant until a month before my visit, when London promoted him to director of development. An aspiring screenwriter, Mahoney is relieved to be moving on from entry level, but always realistic about the hard road both ahead of and behind him. He's seen too many of London's scripts—and a couple of his own—die in development (failing to find traction among prospective studios or financiers) to harbor any illusions.

But he has come quite far since graduating from Arizona State University in 2013. Rather than move to L.A. without any connections, Mahoney went to live near family in New Mexico—a state that happens to be the location for many films and TV shows, thanks to wide-open spaces and generous tax incentives. He did grunt work on several shows, including "dehoarding" a house used for filming by chiseling a rat off the carpet. He calls it "one of those awful experiences that I don't regret," because it helped him make crucial connections. He, too, worked at the Weinstein Company, but in L.A., as an assistant to president David Glasser, a brutally busy job. But when Weinstein collapsed, he came to Groundswell.

Some people can spend six or seven years as assistants before being promoted to full agents, which most agree is not the ideal path. For many assistants, the way to rise up is to find the next job somewhere else, or to find a place small enough that you can pick up more creative tasks and grow into a new title. After a year as the assistant to London's executive partner, Mahoney was promoted to what he considers the most interesting part of production: finding and developing scripts.

"Now I've got to really go out there and have lunches and start meeting people and sourcing material and making my own relationships," says Mahoney. In other words, he's moving out of apprenticeship. The people he meets fall into the category of "baby execs" and "baby agents" (in Hollywood's patronizing shorthand)—those without much more seniority than him. The industry works laterally that way, which makes it difficult to scare up a great script. The best projects tend to be bandied about among senior execs, agents, and producers.

Instead, Mahoney needs to find the overlooked gem. Even at this early phase of his career, he knows better than to expect quick success. That's one reason he's leery of becoming a producer himself. "It's not always glamorous," he says. "You have to manage people and that's fucking hard . . . So many things can go wrong, and everything has to align for something to get on the air. It's moving multiple boulders up the hill and they all have to get there. There's so many opportunities for heartbreak."

Neither Freedman nor Mahoney wants to be a producer like their current boss. And yet they are moving up the rungs of the production ladder. So what separates producers from the thousands of others in the industry who have the savvy and some of the experience, but not the desire?

The producers who succeed, who persist, are those who long to take ownership of a movie in the deepest sense. Obst gets at this essential definition of a producer when she contrasts the job with being an executive, whose responsibility is to the company, and whose success is judged in the aggregate. "As a producer," she says, "your tombstone is filled with your titles." You define the movies and they define you, and in the end you are judged by them. So you'd better make sure they're good.

———

THE LEAP TO ACTUALLY making a project happen is what separates producers from everyone else. It's why none of the producers in this book had anything close to a typical path, because there is none. There are only perseverance and luck, one feeding the other until they come together to create that first improbable success.

The tricky place of the producer in the filmmaking ecosystem—between finance and creative, the system and the artist—is one reason the Sundance Institute decided that producers needed a place to learn, right alongside the directors and screenwriters whose projects they helm. The institute is the educational wing of the Sundance Film Festival, the end-all and be-all of independent festivals.

Every summer since the 1980s, the institute has held intensive filmmaking fellowships in the Wasatch Mountains of Utah. In 2008 they set up a five-day intensive Creative Producing Lab. "We would have a focus for directors and a focus for screenwriters, but there was this third leg of the stool, a very integral part of actually making the film, that we weren't explicitly supporting," says Anne Lai, the founding director of the producing course.

Lai, also a producer, remembers sitting in on a grueling night shoot. "This actor wandered into our area, and he's like, 'You guys don't seem like you're doing anything. You're always just sitting here.'" What, he demanded to know, were they actually doing? Lai was annoyed, but her colleague, a line producer, had an answer: "It's like we're pilots."

Now she considers it a perfect analogy. "We have to put everyone on the plane. We have to get everyone safely off the ground. We have to get to twenty thousand feet. And our job is basically not to crash while you guys do the work that you've all been brought here to do."

Sundance producing fellows come with a project already in hand. Lai's core question to them is one she believes every producer must ask themselves on every project they work on: "What's the urgency for you to make this work? Why do you want to spend time doing it? Because you're not going to get paid very well, it's very much an uphill battle. There must be a reason why you want to devote yourself to it."

The lab is too short to be boot camp or grad school, but in contrast to an agency assistant job, there's no admin. You work on your pitches to investors, your budget and shooting schedule—but especially, Lai says, your presentational and interpersonal skills.

"There has to be an urgency," says Lai, "and it's not because it's important. Because everything's important." An investor or an actor needs to understand why the film is worth putting aside other projects in order to get on board *now*. The ultimate answer to that question can't come from Lai or the senior producers who serve as mentors on the program—and it definitely can't come from the financiers.

One of Lai's success stories is 2016 alum Monique Walton, producer of the indie darling *Bull*, which went on to win recognition at the Cannes Film Festival. Walton was working with a filmmaker, Annie Silverstein, with whom she shared a personal history, an artistic vision, and a long friendship. She and Silverstein had already won a top prize from Cinéfondation, the emerging-artists offshoot of Cannes, for their short film, *Skunk*—a major vote of confidence and a leg up in the eventual scrum for film-festival attention.

Walton fits the mold of the professional-class student who fell in love with film. She was a Latin American studies major at Yale, but while taking a documentary film class she embarked on a project with a friend, about being Black students on a majority-white campus, which they wound up submitting to festivals and touring around the country. "It was great to see how you could have an impact and be in touch with the people who are connected to the film," says Walton. After graduation, she interned for a documentary filmmaker, but eventually she needed to make a living. So she spent a few years at Nick Jr. Online, writing scripts and handling budgets. Finally, she went to film school at the University of Texas at Austin, earning a master's degree in directing, but finding her passion in producing.

"I was directing my own films, but I was producing a lot of my friends' films as well," Walton says. "Even though there wasn't a producing department at film school, everybody needed producing." That's where she met Silverstein, whose senior thesis was *Skunk*—made, Silverstein later said, with "a group of dear friends, a pack of rescue dogs, and two wonderful teenagers." The plot is concise and poignant: two kids set off to recover their stolen pit bull. The Cinéfondation prize at Cannes was bestowed by legendary Iranian filmmaker Abbas Kiarostami, guaranteeing the team a feature film slot at the festival in the future—if they could make a movie.

Bull has some more conventional beats: a troubled Texas teen girl with a mother in jail and no options winds up doing chores for a washed-up veteran of the Black rodeo circuit. She becomes enamored of the rodeo life and spies a way out of her own dead end. An *IndieWire* review concluded that it "stuffs conventional ingredients into a wondrous vision of life on the edge"—a nod to its unusual production process. Walton and Silverstein wanted to use a cast of almost entirely unknown actors, some of them amateurs (with the exception of Rob Morgan, of *Stranger Things* and *This Is Us*, playing the rodeo vet). It would require "lots of bulls and lots of kids," as Walton put it—meaning a lot of on-set hassle. They needed financiers, but they needed those financiers to know what they were in for.

This was where Sundance helped; in preparation for introducing Walton to financiers, the program emphasized the value of knowing what you wanted and asking for it—seeking not just the highest bid but the best match, at the right budget, with the right shooting schedule. Finding producing partners who share your vision is a negotiation that must be performed in good faith—not an easy thing to master when you're young, you've sunk personal savings into a passion project, and you feel that everything is riding on the green light that only money can provide.

A couple of months after the summer lab, Walton participated in Sundance's Catalyst program, which invites alumni to present their projects before dozens of financiers for a shot at finding (and funding) the next great talent. Some meetings were awkward; many financiers weren't interested in paying for forty days of filming an iffy commercial proposition when the typical indie shoot was ten days shorter. The producers managed to filter for those who were serious very quickly. "We were able to tell what they were interested in and what they wanted to support, and out of that came someone who eventually became our majority investor."

When a producer has enough financing in place to start signing contracts with production teams, actors, designers, carpenters, and so many more members of the small army it takes to make even the smallest professional movie, it's time to head into preproduction. This is when the details are hammered out, the project becomes real, and there's no turning back.

3

THE PHENOM

Siena Oberman joined a table of producers and agents at the San Vicente Bungalows, a members-only club in West Hollywood that has recently become the chief watering hole of the industry. With its lush California foliage playing against Hamptons luxe interior design and its $56 expense-account hamburgers, the Bungalows is the kind of place where they make you tape over your cell phone camera. But it's known less for the celebrities you might be able to spy on (though there are some) than the deals you're likely to overhear.

On this particular autumn evening, Oberman is describing preparations to film *The Birthday Cake* in New York, where she'll travel in a few weeks to begin preproduction. "It's a mob movie set in present-day Brooklyn," she explains, in quiet pitch mode. "A modern-day twist on the mob genre. Our writers interviewed New York locals arrested for different mob crimes. It's really about the culture clash between the old and new Brooklyn."

Anne Lai at the Sundance Institute was not the only producer to compare her job to that of an airline pilot. When Oberman gets into some of the financing complications, her confidence flags—prompting one producer to say over her martini, "You're two weeks out and you're moving up the runway and you're not sure if you have enough fuel!"

Oberman laughs. It's both true and inevitable. She has worked tirelessly to secure funding for the indie film—has already shot a day of footage in L.A. featuring the biggest actors (Ewan McGregor, Lorraine Bracco), whose presence helped persuade foreign sales agents to guarantee much of the budget. In other words, sales projections got the airplane on the runway, and it's gaining speed. There's plenty of fuel to take off and plenty more guaranteed, but commitments alone won't land the plane.

Oberman doesn't seem too troubled by this—her calm is a steady state, especially here at the Bungalows—but when we meet again in New York, in a boutique hotel not far from her temporary East Village production office, she displays the hyper-alertness of someone whose toddler is wandering at the edge of a pool.

"Honestly, every time I'm in preproduction I wish we had more time," she says. "Cash flow and cast agreements should always close sooner than they do, it's just the reality of indie producing." She's still waiting for money that is contractually owed to arrive, some of which the film needs urgently. Without the timely wiring of money, the crew can start to get antsy, and in a worst-case scenario, the production could get shut down. She might have to ask the powerful Screen Actors Guild for an extension the following day.

"I've never had a movie fall apart during production," Oberman says. "I've definitely *felt* like it was going to fall apart. Almost every movie close to production feels like it's going to fall apart because there's still deal-breaking moments to get through in prep. Even today, my state of mind is, 'I *think* I'm making a movie in a week?' It doesn't hit me as fully real until everything is locked in and we're on set."

The fear is not so much of personal failure as of letting others down when they most need the work—when they most need her. "We have a certain amount of money, and we have a certain amount more coming in, but we have a team of about one hundred people that I have to go see in the office, talk to on the phone, and tell them they have jobs for the next two months when I'm simply, to some extent, going off my own due diligence, our attorney's due diligence, and contractual commitments. Technically, it could fall apart if not handled properly."

It may seem odd to say about someone under thirty, but with thirteen producer credits to her name, Oberman has enough experience and knowledge to put a potential crisis in perspective. "In producing, anything and everything can go wrong; it's the producer's job to fix it and keep the team together, even under the constant threat that the movie could collapse. What I've learned is to just stay calm, or as calm as possible."

It's hard to avoid broadening the analogy of the half-fueled plane to the career arcs of most producers, which depend on circumstances outside one's control and can only achieve liftoff with a healthy dose of hubris. It applies especially to Oberman's path, which is far from typical, born of equal parts talent and grit, luck and misfortune.

Oberman grew up in Palos Verdes, a comfortable ocean-side suburb of Los Angeles, the daughter of a nurse and a father who worked in live events. His career never touched on movies, but Oberman's high school had a well-funded film program.

"It was the only elective that allowed you to go off

campus," says Oberman. "So I thought, 'Oh sweet, I can leave class and go to the beach.' I wasn't necessarily interested in film my freshman year, but through this class we got to make short films with friends, and I became obsessed with writing, filming, directing, and editing."

She fell in love with movies, too, particularly high-art thrillers by Christopher Nolan and David Fincher. "I remember writing as many film papers in school as I could on *Se7en*, watching it over and over again, each time finding more details." It explains her particular penchant as a producer for psychological thrillers with social components wedded to sophisticated cinematography.

Oberman was an all-around go-getter; she volunteered for the Red Cross and wound up on their National Youth Council, boosting the nonprofit's youth outreach through social media and even helping make a commercial with Disney. She won a Volunteer of the Year Award. When her work raised youth volunteer sign-ups nationwide, "I realized the power of the media."

And though she fell in love with film, she didn't exactly fall into the field. "I thought I wanted to be a doctor, but I couldn't pass AP Bio," she says. "So it was kind of like, what do I like and then what am I best at?" In high school she was focused on directing, and she made twenty short films. As soon as Oberman started college at Loyola Marymount University, just up the bay, she began exploring every film internship she could find—essentially fast-tracking the assistant experience. During college she assembled a résumé more varied than many careers: IM Global, an international film sales firm; Route One Entertainment, an indie production and finance company; Plan B, Brad Pitt's Oscar-winning production company; Paramount Pictures; and UTA.

By her sophomore year, Oberman had an inkling of what producing was. She interviewed with the CEO of Warner Bros. "He told me if I wanted to be successful, I needed to get really good at one thing, instead of trying to be a jack-of-all-trades—and then, once I succeeded, I could expand into other things more easily." She took his advice to heart. "I focused on what came most naturally, which was producing."

All the while, Oberman was taking her short films to festivals, including Cannes and Outfest, meeting producers, directors, actors, and financiers and building up a Rolodex that would make her a formidable connector of money and talent by the time she was able to drink legally. She transferred to USC, pursuing dual degrees in the university's business and film schools. She finished her business degree but left the film program because she became too busy helping produce two films. One of these was part of a graduate production course taught by James Franco.

All of this helped prepare Oberman for producing, to be sure, but it wasn't what set her career track to warp speed. In her senior year, Oberman had a pinched nerve in her back. A doctor botched what should have been a simple procedure and broke one of her vertebrae. The injury required two more surgeries and hobbled her on and off for two years. She could still travel and talk on the phone, but she couldn't sit at a desk for an entire day. Her plan to become an assistant at an agency was derailed. It might have been the best thing that happened to her so far.

"I went to a lot of festivals, did general meetings with tons of people, and asked them for advice," she says. "I had a lot of time on my hands, which I spent researching the business and consuming films. I thought, *I'll try and make another feature and then get a normal job.* But I couldn't physically get a normal job. I was extremely frustrated, but I had to learn to embrace it and make the most out of what I could do in my situation—which was freelance producing."

She recognizes how improbable it was. "The idea that

I'm going to go get famous actors and millions of dollars and suddenly 'be a producer' at twenty-two? I don't think I would ever have been brave enough to pursue it myself because it's kind of crazy." But she felt she had no other choice.

Oberman still needed money while she built up her credits, so she relied on her strengths by doing financing—essentially acting as a bridge between investors and producers. Taking a fee of around 5 percent, Oberman had enough stability to try producing. She eased into it by coming under the wing of a finance and production company called Yale Productions as a development executive. They gave her a base salary with bumps along the way for financing and for completing films. She helped get four made in a year and pulled in six figures.

Financing was a quicker way to make a living, but it wasn't enough for her. "There is such a misconception that producing is inherently lucrative," she says. Sure, the upside is great at higher levels. But it takes many years and low-paying passion projects to get there. "If I simply wanted to make money, I would focus on quick finance deals, as opposed to immersive producing, where each project occupies years of my life." One *Birthday Cake* per year would barely exceed the annual minimum wage in California.

After a year at Yale Productions, Oberman had enough connections, experience, and cash to survive on her own. One of the movies she'd made with Yale, *Burn*, featured Shiloh Fernandez, whom she'd met earlier in a writers' meeting. He was developing his own passion project with two cowriters—an indie mob movie that needed a producer to help develop it, and negotiate the finance deals in order to get the movie green-lit. Raul Bermudez, the producer and cowriter of *The Birthday Cake*, was casting about for producers, he told me, when "Shiloh said, 'I know this girl, she's young and ambitious.' "

Bermudez checked her out and spoke with her, and he was quickly sold. "We're not a conventional project—first-time director, and we needed more than our lead actor to greenlight the movie. So you need someone who's gonna fight for it like I was gonna fight for it. Siena, she understood what we were trying to do. So here we are."

IT's BEEN A FEW weeks since Oberman and I met and discussed the half-fueled plane of her mob drama *The Birthday Cake*, which has since lifted off but taken some detours. The filming in New York is tightly focused on a couple of atmospheric locations, but it has also been fragmented, working around yet another person's schedule. For all its on-screen cameos, the film has a lot of first-time talent behind the camera: Director Jimmy Giannopoulos is a music producer, well known for his band LOLAWOLF (with Zoë Kravitz), but this is his feature directorial debut. Co-creator Raul Bermudez and executive producer Greg Lauritano have worked on only a few features prior to this (though they aren't new to the industry).

Sean Price Williams, the cinematographer, is another story. A highly regarded indie legend, acclaimed for the Safdie brothers' *Good Time* and the more recent *Tesla*, he was brought on for his deft touch and indie-documentary style. ("He's the lead actor in my mind," Giannopoulos told me.) Unfortunately, Williams was so much in demand that he had to shoot a short film in Madagascar in November. And so *The Birthday Cake* was prepped and shot in stutter step: preproduction for weeks, followed by a week of shooting in mid-November, another week of prep, a week off for Thanksgiving, and then a grueling two-week stretch in December—six-day weeks with many cold outdoor night shoots.

As any producer will tell you, talent is the essential element of any production. "You can make a bad movie with a great director," says Lynda Obst, "but you can't make a great movie with a bad director." Accommodating that talent is usually worth the extra trouble—which is not to say there isn't extra trouble, especially when dealing with a limited indie budget.

We are now into Thursday of the movie's first December week, and the borrowed Italianate house will host the climactic scene of the movie: Gio, the protagonist played by Shiloh Fernandez, comes to a feast with his uncles on the tenth anniversary of his father's death—a memorial meal that will end very dramatically. An assortment of swaggering (male) actors will be crowding a house that seems spacious for a single family but not a full crew, an ensemble cast, and a tight setup. The clamorous conclusion will be shot tomorrow. Today is all about rising tension.

So it is for the producers, too—albeit with less violent results. The wacky shoot schedule has thrown the crew a bit off-balance. "It felt like thirty different films," says Heliya Alam, an associate producer who walks me over to the set from "holding," the production's current base camp in the basement of a nearby church. "But it helped us because we were still casting a few supporting roles."

There is also, of course, the money. As Alam and I arrive

on set, Oberman is still in Manhattan, trying to figure out why she can't get ahold of a portion of one investor's money until two weeks from now, and why it has to come from the Isle of Man, a tax shelter off the coast of England. In this case, the filming delay actually helps. To extend the pilot analogy, this plane has had a couple of layovers, which is handy if your fuel won't arrive until the next stop.

The extended shoot has also allowed time for some financiers to visit. There will be five such "executive producers" on set today—two of whom Oberman has never met—and more the following week. Some are direct investors; others are financiers' employees. One EP who works for a financier is already on set when we arrive: Fernando Ferro of Foton Pictures, an international company based in Miami. We head down together into the basement of the house, which is serving as a bare-bones version of what's often called Video Village—the area where those who don't have to be on set (or can't fit) watch the shoot on monitors.

Ferro and his team helped out with initial financing of the picture, but will also be involved in postproduction, sales, and distribution. He's been visiting for a few days, and he likes what he sees. "It's very telling for the movie, the atmosphere on set," he says. "It's diverse, it's young, everyone's hungry to make something. Anyone who tells you production is easy-breezy, that's bullshit. But it's not about the bullshit that happens. It's how the producer responds and how that trickles down."

He believes Oberman's even temperament is her greatest asset. "Siena—and you can print this—she's going to be one of the top-tier producers in our industry. We're lucky because we got to know her before everyone else did."

As if on cue, Oberman comes down into the basement, greeting everyone with a calm smile. Fresh off a forty-five-minute Uber ride, she's just stopping in to say hello, planning on heading back to "holding" at the church to greet two more EPs. After introducing herself to a couple of other guests, she starts to realize how crowded the house is becoming. Another item for her to-do list.

Oberman has a quick conversation with Ferro about the eventual press package—its design and titles and behind-the-scenes footage. Then Alam pulls her aside to tell her that rehearsals are up, and Val is about to begin. Decades after *Top Gun* made him famous, Kilmer survived a battle with throat cancer, requiring a tracheotomy. He speaks with the help of a breathing device—something that's been worked into his character: Uncle Angelo had once been shot.

This is one of Val's first roles since recovering from cancer, which feels momentous and exciting for all involved. He's charming and spry, astonishingly fit and good-natured. His long hair, weathered face, and intense commitment suit the role perfectly—entirely aside from the added value of a movie star in an indie film. One of the producer's most important jobs is to make any actor feel safe and respected on set.

Another dilemma is brought to the producer's attention: Kilmer has brought along a documentary production team (he's filming a biography about his journey). There's a little bit of space on the third floor, a large converted attic that serves as his dressing room. But there's not enough room in the house for a second production team.

It's easy to forget, in the flurry of all these other tasks, that Oberman is ostensibly overseeing the actual footage of the day. But before even considering aesthetics, she needs to figure out how to get Kilmer's producer to sign a nondisclosure agreement. She needs to be sure that scenes of *The Birthday Cake* aren't leaked, and she also has to speak with crew members who may not want to appear in an entirely separate movie on top of their intense day of production. And she still needs to handle the money stuck in the Isle of Man.

She also needs to free up more space in the house. In this case, one problem solves another. Paul Sorvino has been unexpectedly delayed, forcing the team to rearrange its shooting schedule, but it also means Sorvino's basement dressing room is available. She asks a crew member to set it up with a monitor or, failing that, a Wi-Fi hookup so people can watch the filming on their phones.

"I just want to say hi to one of the EPs," she says, leaving the house and heading up the block. "He just flew in yesterday." The minute we cross the street, they are in sight. Damiano and Tiziano Tucci were connected to Oberman via Endeavor Content, an innovative studio affiliated with WME that will act as the film's sales agent. The Tucci brothers have funded a significant amount of the film's budget without ever laying eyes on its lead producers. "I've never given money to a project without first meeting the people, except her," says Damiano.

We head upstairs to watch some filming, before being chased out by a PA: "Guys, way too many people in here, I'm very sorry. We have plenty of space downstairs!" And the producers are thereby chased off their own set.

Oberman finally settles the EPs into Sorvino's room, onto a futon flanked by old exercise equipment. They can't connect to the camera feed via Wi-Fi, though; someone needs to find out the house password.

Oberman walks outside to confer about two pressing, parallel problems: First, one department head is growing frustrated with the proliferation of guests on set. And second, mistakes made by another crew member have been costing them money and time.

Oberman deals first with the department head. "It feels like no one is listening," he says. Oberman listens as he describes a series of miscommunications, but she never turns up the heat. She proposes solutions, improvised but reasonable. They'll send out an email mandating one pre-announced guest per day. She'll run the NDAs up to Kilmer and his team herself—and email them, too. They'll require the documentary crew (except for one videographer) to wait in the car during shooting.

Lauritano joins the conversation and agrees that they should establish stronger rules. Then he and Oberman step aside to confer on the counterproductive crew member. They decide to quietly remove his responsibilities and dole them out among themselves and Alam. They agree to have a larger team meeting at lunch to get a sign-off from the line producer and Bermudez. Oberman tasks Lauritano with making sure Kilmer's team doesn't do any filming until the NDAs are signed.

Back in the house, Oberman spends a few minutes on set, and soon comes down to the basement with good news: Kilmer is having the time of his life—dramatically practicing the violent climax—and the filmmakers are happy with his performance. He offered to let them have as much footage of him as they need for a behind-the-scenes feature. Which is good, because Oberman had just found out the sales agents are asking for that footage to court foreign distributors. And with that, an announcement is made. It's time for lunch.

The meal break, featuring a hot buffet in the church basement of "holding," is a large, communal affair, made more communal by the presence of a couple hundred senior citizens taking up half the space for a very loud bingo game. As locals call out winning letters and numbers, the producers ladle food onto their plates alongside the crew and chat for a few minutes, before gathering in a far corner to grapple with the most hectic day of production so far.

Giannopoulos comes by to sing Oberman's praises. "Siena, she's fucking cool," he says. "She's focused, and she trusted us all the way, you know what I mean? All the way.

She's never told me I can't do something. I say I want some-thing and they make it happen." That's what a producer's job really entails: Making the project stronger by support-ing the artist's vision while doing what's best, in practical terms, for the art.

After their meeting, the producers take a table and con-tinue to work. As the meal winds down and the bingo picks up steam, Oberman talks to one of the financiers about a chunk of their money that's been delayed; an associate with a family emergency was supposed to have kicked in over a hundred grand. On the way back to set, she says she is frus-trated at having to handle so many of the logistics on her own: "I'm managing production workflow and financing, but I would prefer to be watching every take of each scene. It's just not exactly what we planned, but you have to adapt to the needs of each day of production."

Oberman does eventually get to have some creative input. After lunch, Paul Sorvino arrives on set, and the more intensive filming begins. There's a mandated safety demonstration involving a prop gun. The room is fogged up to create a hazy lighting effect, giving the digital shoot a cinematic tinge. The scene that gets the most focus is one in which an uncle, played by William Fichtner, confronts Gio.

Fichtner, playing a corrupt cop, eases into the scene, plays with the words, lets his swagger and menace grow.

It's a bravura sequence, but as Oberman watches in the basement, she is concerned. "Have they done any wides yet?" she asks a crew member. "It's tight." A producer always needs to think about the eventual edit, to make sure they have enough shot options for cutting a movie long after they'll be able to shoot anything new. A scene heavy on close-ups might just need an extra transition or two.

Ferro says they're probably getting it. "I think they're just trying to lock in that choreography."

"They will," says Oberman, "but I should check in."

She runs upstairs and talks to the cinematographer and director. "I don't say anything unless I think they're missing something," she tells me later. "I like to say, 'If you never use it, that's okay, but it's good to have options in the edit.'" Jimmy Giannopoulos is a prolific music producer, but this is his directorial debut. Creative producers like Bermudez and Oberman have to think about how the scenes will work together on every film, but especially with a director new to this process.

Oberman can be firm with her notes but she doesn't sell; she offers options. When she doesn't want to prod, she nudges. Later, she tells me about a table read on a different script still in progress. She was disappointed that the readers were visibly bored at times but offered little criticism. "I said, 'So when did you guys feel like it was slow?' And they pointed out one moment, but it should have been four." If she felt so strongly about four exact moments, why didn't she just give the notes herself? "I wanted the writer to hear it from other people, not me."

The fact that Oberman hasn't offered many such notes on this particular day is just a function of the project. "There are so many artists watching the creative" on this shoot, she says as we leave the house and head back to the church. "Our weaker spot is that we don't have as big a logistics team. I have to prevent the movie from falling apart first, then focus on making it the best it can be second, since I have strong creative partners. On different movies it's different priorities, depending on the team."

Back at the church, Oberman checks her phone and hears a message in Spanish from the financier whose money is stuck in the Isle of Man. She can only make out a few key phrases: "It's not possible . . . two to three weeks . . . can't do it." She decides that, since she can use that money for post-production, she can wait it out. She engages with Lauritano in a mind-numbing discussion of the numbers required for the tax-credit loan, before tabling a final proofread of those numbers until the morning.

Sitting down at one of the bingo tables, Oberman takes out her task list, which she's been rubbing like a talisman. "So this is my to-do list for today," she says. "I didn't get through a ton of it, but I made it last night so I could go to sleep calmer." When she looks down, though, she brightens a little. "A lot of it we did." She points to different groupings on the page. "These are all production concerns. These are all current financiers, these are potentials in case anything goes wrong. This is just legal. But like: 'Weather, continuity; money out of Isle of Man; post equity, deliverables; Endeavor response; tracking board.' And we need to find an editor. That's something to focus on, something none of us have been able to focus on. We had an editor in preproduction but it didn't end up being the right fit, so we need to start the search again."

As it nears 8 p.m., she says goodbye to some stragglers and starts to head out herself when she sees a call: the COO of the financing company with the missing hundred grand. Explaining the problem to him, she smoothly interweaves reassurances with alarm over what might happen if the money doesn't come through near enough to its scheduled slot in the cash flow (payroll will collapse, SAG will fine them, the crew will mutiny, they won't be able to file the proper tax paperwork). I ask how the call went. She shrugs and says she'll find out later. She's done all she can.

SEVERAL WEEKS AFTER THE shoot, Oberman is more relaxed. She managed to take a long trip to Hawaii. "I was burned out," she says. The money from the challenging investor had come through after all; the Isle of Man money was winding its way to America. And Oberman was already thinking ahead to other projects.

She'd been perusing the Black List, an annual publication of the best unproduced screenplays, which are subject to fierce competition among indie producers (past entries include *Argo*, *The King's Speech*, and *Juno*). Her goal was to grow into bigger budget ranges as a lead producer while supporting more indie films as an EP. She wanted to continue to build out her trusted teams and networks—producing partners, financiers, and crews that she could rely on, film after film.

As the fog of *The Birthday Cake* began to clear, she

was thinking about how to become better valued for her work, to wield more influence despite not conforming to the archetype of the older, male producer. There was one film she'd been working on with a production company she knew well. "They said, 'Oh, we need to bring on a lead producer.' And I've been helping them for free for six months—developed the script, brought in financing, helped them with the cast. But I knew they weren't going with me, so I referred them to some guy friends." Their eventual pick had less producing experience than her—and none with that movie.

Yet the financiers and producers who know Oberman already talk about her as a rising star—a circle that gets bigger every day. As Ferro, the EP, had said, the more talent and producers she works with, the more of them will know.

One slightly bigger-budget film Oberman worked on recently was *Mainstream*, a satire set in the world of social media starring Andrew Garfield and Maya Hawke. She teamed up for that one with Fred Berger. Berger too had made the producer/pilot analogy, and he was speaking from experience; after years of taxiing on the runway, he's flying with a lot more fuel now. Berger has already attained the budget level that Oberman and so many younger producers hope to crack one day. He has a robust management production company, complete with managers and development specialists and more than one attorney to support him and his partners. He has put in his time in the trenches, and he has had his breaks, lucky and unlucky, along the always-atypical path to becoming a successful producer.

4

THE PERFECTIONIST

You may recognize Fred Berger from the historic debacle of the 2017 Academy Awards, when *La La Land* was initially—and erroneously—announced as the winner for Best Picture. Berger and the other producers each gave their speeches before finding out that, in fact, *Moonlight* had won.

Though that journey didn't quite have a storybook ending, Berger is happy to talk about *La La Land*, the improbable box-office hit, a musical love letter to Los Angeles, that capped a seven-year period of impoverished struggle and set him on the course of a more lucrative struggle he follows today.

In 2016, just as Berger was strategizing *La La Land*'s release, he joined the growing production company Automatik as a partner to prolific producer Brian Kavanaugh-Jones. Many production companies attach themselves to either an equity investor or a studio; Automatik shares offices with its sister company Grandview, a management firm. Producing ten to fifteen movies a year, Berger and Kavanaugh-Jones are working their way up from indie darlings to big-budget powers—from films almost as small as *The Birthday Cake* to upcoming projects that include several major biopics, a trio of VFX-heavy sci-fi features, and a groundbreaking, big-budget streaming thriller series, all for studios and streamers.

In the fall of 2019, I visited Berger's L.A. office, hearing the backstories of films about which details will be obscured at Berger's request. I watched as he encountered all of the creative producer's stations of the cross: script development, negotiation, talent packaging, preproduction, and marketing; petitioning for money and gathering valuable intelligence.

I met Berger for the first time in New York at the Bowery Hotel. At 11 a.m., he was still groggy. Not only was he on L.A. time, he'd been up half the night negotiating the complex sale of a film on which parties strongly disagreed, watching the latest cut of another film, and reading a script in advance of a meeting with the writer. Nonetheless, as he downed espressos, he accelerated to warp speed in describing his life so far.

Berger's father was born in Cairo, but his family left

Egypt during the expulsion of the Jewish community when Berger's father was a teenager. He wound up in New York, where he met Berger's mother, a French woman getting her MBA at Cornell. Together they started a business importing baby furniture. Fred grew up in the heart of a classic first-generation story: entrepreneurial parents toiling in a trade so their children could grow up to be professionals. He describes his father as "a political junkie . . . a person with many passions, but he didn't have the luxury of making a dream-driven choice."

As a teenager, Berger would join his parents at furniture trade shows, assembling and hawking cribs. "It was a stark lesson for me in several ways," he says. "One was work ethic, which my parents instilled in us very early. My brother and I never bought anything with money we hadn't earned. Another was taking pride in our work. My mom's favorite saying (in French) was, 'If it deserves to be done, it deserves to be done well.' And finally, I didn't want my work to be a 'job'—merely earning a living, counting the hours till the day ends." He treasured his parents' sacrifice, and he's deeply grateful for the opportunities it afforded him, but he saw that they were not inspired by their work. "I was determined to do something I was passionate about."

Still, at the University of Pennsylvania, he was torn between his aesthetic impulses and his family's drive for stability. Majoring in PPE (Philosophy, Politics, and Economics), which was sort of a pre-law curriculum, he considered law school, but his love for movies kept intruding. He didn't know where to take that passion, exactly. "I had no connections to the business," he says. "Writing, I was okay, but it was torture, like homework. I was a terrible actor." He thought about directing. And like most would-be filmmakers, he didn't have much of a concept of what "producing" meant. He did a few internships in college, "and each one just sucked me in deeper and deeper."

Berger had caught the movie bug in high school. It began with photography and film history courses and ended with him running the local TV station. He was also deeply influenced by the last golden age of indie cinema. "Everyone hails the seventies, which were no doubt exceptional, but for my money, the nineties were the best decade of American cinema," he says, describing it as a moment when the industry's economics, coupled with popular consumption, allowed rising filmmakers to operate with unbridled ambition.

"The budgets for bold auteur-driven movies are almost inconceivable today—though the streamers are thankfully changing that. When you think of Tarantino, Spike Lee, Paul Thomas Anderson, Kathryn Bigelow, Ang Lee, David Fincher, Alexander Payne, and on and on—so many of our current icons were painting on a big canvas during the nineties. For me, as a teenager, it was an abundance of riches." It was art wedded to high production values. "Look at *Good Will Hunting*, which I just rewatched. That was an 'indie movie,' yet there are huge aerial shots of Boston and abundant extras. Today, that's a $4 million Sundance movie, shot in twenty-two days."

We'll get to the tectonic shifts in independent film-making later; suffice it to say that Berger was inspired. He wanted to be as close to the filmmaking process as possible, figure out how everything functioned. During college, he interned for a start-up distribution company, ThinkFilm, in New York—"totally broke, waiting tables on the off days while commuting to the city from Westchester to be the first one in, last one out, for free. I loved every second of it."

The city's indie film scene was in its "glory days," mostly concentrated in the downtown Manhattan neighborhood of Tribeca. "I was calling small theaters for grosses every Monday. I would go around the city, begging restaurant owners to let me tape movie fliers to their windows." Several prominent filmmakers called the office and Berger was starstruck. "In the smallest way, I felt the fourth wall come down." Berger had dreamed of "being part of a team that made movies that inspired other people the way movies had inspired me." For the first time, an industry career felt attainable.

"I was told my entire life that a career in film was 'impossible' or 'too hard,' " he says. "But I tell younger people today: Don't listen to those voices. If you're passionate, driven, and can't conceive of doing anything else, there is room for you."

After graduation, he was referred by his friends at ThinkFilm to an internship at Focus Features just in time to participate in reshoots on *Eternal Sunshine of the Spotless Mind*—in fact, to appear in it. The tallest production assistant around, he served as Jim Carrey's stand-in for a few insert shots. His hand is in the movie. "A year earlier, I was devouring Charlie Kaufman and Michel Gondry films. Suddenly I'm in a car, in Jim Carrey's wardrobe, with Gondry directing, and Ellen Kuras shooting." He was so nervous that he almost crashed the car.

"What I'm describing," he says, "are the little incidents of the bug, the addiction, where you get a small taste for the creative process and crave more. There's an enormous amount of pain, struggle, conflict, and disappointment in this business, but if movies are the dream, being even a tiny cog in the wheel is the highest high you can imagine."

He got his first real job assisting producer Ross Katz, who by his early thirties had already been twice Oscar-nominated (*In the Bedroom*, *Lost in Translation*). Berger's big break as Katz's assistant was traveling to Paris for Sofia Coppola's *Marie Antoinette*. In practice, this meant driving top talent between chateaus and attending to their needs. It was exhausting and exhilarating, and it helped him earn the trust of people at the top of the indie world. He wound up supervising postproduction on the movie. When Katz decided to direct a movie, a Kevin Bacon vehicle for HBO called *Taking Chance*, Berger helped produce, earning his first credit in 2009. It would be seven years before his next one.

"Luck is such a huge factor," Berger reflects. "Anyone who discounts luck in their success is destined for a rude awakening. If Sofia had decided to make her next movie in Prague, I wouldn't have been there. Because I was French, I could be uniquely useful. It was formative for me. Who knows where I'd be without that experience?"

This isn't to imply that success for a producer is just a

series of lucky breaks. "The harder you work, the luckier you get," he says. "But it's vital to recognize the people and opportunities that pave the way to your success—and to remember that for every win, a loss could easily be around the corner."

A case in point: shortly afterward, he made what might have been a dumb and costly mistake. He had already become Katz's producing partner, but when Katz transitioned into writing and directing full-time, Berger decided to go out on his own rather than take a job with another producer as a development executive.

Going back to his pilot analogy, "I unhooked from the plane while still on the runway, without enough momentum to justify going out alone." But after years of autonomy and immersion in the creative process, it was hard to swallow the idea of subordinating himself to someone else's creative mandate and abdicating hands-on producing to a boss. "It was just a stupid, arrogant point of view," he says. But he was also following advice given to him by Coppola and others: "Take a big leap, at the right time, even if it's scary. I was in the wilderness for years. But it ended up working out."

Berger started to develop ideas, which, lacking big names behind them, sat around for years. Yet they provided valuable lessons and enduring connections. One project was *Strange but True*, adapted from a John Searles novel by Eric Garcia in 2008—now an old friend and a partner on a much bigger project in the works. (*Strange but True* was finally released in 2019.) There was also *The Autopsy of Jane Doe*, an indie horror that earned several awards and has become a cult classic. And another, of course, was *La La Land*.

"The filming of *La La Land* was a magical experience," says Berger. "The path to getting it made was absolute hell, the most harrowing experience of my life. As a producer, you're defenseless without currency or infrastructure, especially when your project turns from something no one wants into something everyone wants."

Berger met director Damien Chazelle through a friend when Chazelle was twenty-five and Berger twenty-nine. The idea of an original movie musical seemed bold, unprecedented, and an impossible sell.

"At the time, original musicals were dead, and no one wanted to see a movie about actors, or jazz, and least of all a love letter to L.A.," says Berger. "People passed on the movie for six years. Hard no. One studio's notes on the script warned that it would destroy the musical genre." But what Berger and his partner, producer Jordan Horowitz, were gambling on was a great script and the audacious young talent behind it. The talent paid off in spades when Chazelle's earlier movie, *Whiplash*—an equally improbable success about a sadistic drumming instructor—started building buzz. The movie went on to win three Oscars in 2015. And Hollywood, predictably, turned on a dime. "I was with Damien at Sundance when overnight my shy, modest friend turned into a superstar. Suddenly, everyone's in the mix."

Chazelle's success created its own problems, teaching Berger about just how precarious a producer's position can be. Powerful producers with studio connections began circling, trying to edge out Berger and Horowitz, the young Westchester boys who had been producing the film from the start. "We survived, because of an unshakable bond between Damien, Jordan, and myself—and a conviction that we had to protect Damien's vision."

Some producers might have pushed to make the movie into something they felt was more overtly commercial, but Chazelle, Berger, and Horowitz believed the commercial potential of the movie *depended* on its uniqueness—from the opening number on the freeway to the melancholy dream-ballet ending. "The movie never tested well. There was all sorts of pressure to change the ending or tighten the pacing. We did solicit and listen to quite a bit of feedback. But there were certain red lines we fought for through to the end."

The low point may have been when Emma Watson and *Whiplash* star Miles Teller both dropped out after the film had been green-lit by Lionsgate, the film's studio. At that point, partly to reassure the studio, the filmmakers invited veteran producer Marc Platt, who had some experience making musicals (*Wicked*, *Into the Woods*) as well as bigger prestige movies (*Bridge of Spies*), to join the team.

"It was one of the best decisions we made," says Berger. "Filmmaking can't be about ego. A movie is a baby, and you have to build the best family to nurture it." Platt's involvement helped give stars Emma Stone and Ryan Gosling the confidence to come aboard—and Lionsgate the comfort to let Chazelle pursue the film he wanted to make.

"Going back to luck," Berger says, "there were years where I was utterly convinced the movie would never happen. Ultimately, I still can't believe the confluence of fortune that led to our dream version of the movie."

La La Land may have lost Best Picture, but it did earn a record seven Golden Globes and six Oscars, including one for Chazelle, the youngest director ever to win. Only *Titanic* and *All About Eve* have received as many nominations—fourteen. And *La La Land* will soon close in on a half-billion dollars in worldwide box office. All in all, a decent bet for a young producer, for whom seven years of obscurity were well worth the trouble.

BUZZING INTO THE OFFICES of Automatik and Grandview, in the La Brea section of L.A., is a jarring experience. The headquarters are in a squat building above an old-school kosher bakery. Upstairs through a back entrance, though, is a cavernous lobby of poured concrete, mod couches, and skylit ceilings—Bushwick, Brooklyn, by way of a boutique hotel. Inside, on the way to Fred Berger's office, a row of Edison light bulbs hangs from a shiny exposed-pipe ceiling, with the reception area separated from the main hall by a divider of braided twine. Dominating Berger's office is an L-shaped table of unfinished wood.

Berger's assistant, sitting just outside his glass-walled office, gets in early, but the producer himself takes calls from home many mornings. Since he rarely gets home before 7 or 8 p.m., it gives him precious time with his toddler. Which is not to say he isn't working.

Later, in his office, Berger gave me the broad strokes of a day that was typical only in its frenetic pace. This particular day began at home at 8 a.m. He'd been working with a first-time creator to develop a dance-driven movie—a project dear to the heart of a producer who launched his career on a film that helped revive that very genre. So, he and the creator got on the phone with a company that could foot the bill for a first-draft script—essentially the "development" stage.

The creator focused on the mood of the piece and made references to art films that didn't have huge box office. Berger supplemented the pitch with some more-commercial references, focused on the lighter notes and emotional wallops. Warming up with a couple espressos, he made an emotive appeal to the power of movies: "We are deeply compelled by proficiency on-screen, whether it be dancing in *Black Swan*, singing in *Walk the Line*, fighting in the *Bourne* movies, or ice-skating in *I, Tonya*. We also naturally empathize with underdogs. The more the world tells a character they don't belong or can't succeed, the more we root for our protagonists to prove them wrong. All of these things are useful narrative tropes."

After the call, Berger and the creator followed up with a side call to assess how it went. Throughout the day, this is the producer's pattern: a big call with the studio, financiers, and reps, involving maybe a half dozen people, preceded or followed by a prep or postmortem with creative partners. Hollywood runs on a round-robin of overlapping phone calls, in which interests are aligned, teams built, and pitches carefully calibrated.

I ask Berger how likely it is that the movie will be made. He is, as ever, realistic. "I consider every movie unlikely at this phase, given everything that has to go right. But that doesn't deter us if we believe in it." Most of his projects started out unlikely, he adds, and the hard ones often have the biggest potential.

Berger is moving away from smaller movies that can be impossible to get off the ground. "This year Brian and I have *Bad Education* and *Seberg* on the festival circuit, movies we're enormously proud of." They starred Hugh Jackman and Kristen Stewart, respectively.

There's a long tradition in Hollywood of big-name actors alternating blockbusters with projects on which they're willing to take pay cuts in return for artistic fulfillment. There's even a common phrase for it: "One for me, one for them." (The "them" being the studios.) Berger's last couple of years have been taken up with a number of prestige "one for me" projects—the type of films that can make a lasting impact and, if all the pieces fall into place, win major awards.

But that is slowly changing for Berger; like many producers who've reached acclaim with smaller projects, he is aiming for bigger-budget pictures. "We'll always gravitate to execution-dependent films," by which he means movies that don't have the security of a well-known IP, like *Marvel* or obvious blockbuster concepts—that can't survive on B-plus execution. "But we're ready to play in a bigger landscape with more resources and wider distribution."

A little later that morning one such project got a boost, and it puts a spring in his step as he enters the office. He's been trying for more than a year to put together a high-profile biopic, and he's gotten the news that the talent team is finally coming together. "The director's written the majority of the script and it's incredible," he says. He just has one ancillary phone call to make; a potential cast member is shooting another movie that might overlap with this project, and Berger needs to know for sure that the actor will be available.

He calls up the head of the studio—makes the kind of subtle information exchange the industry thrives on. He describes it to me as a bit of a dance, or a highly improvised chess match. "This is a very social business," Berger says. "I needed information from him, but he wanted some from me before he gave it, so I had to give him some of what he wanted but not so much that I got in trouble." And, after twenty minutes of jockeying, he got what he needed; the shoots wouldn't overlap.

Next up was a much more detail-oriented phone call, part of a deeply immersive process of the kind that Berger revels in—the "budget pass" on a sci-fi script—in which certain elements had to be changed to reduce the projected budget: more practical vs. CGI effects; fewer actors and locations; fewer helicopters and more SUVs.

An experienced screenwriter knows she's writing toward a certain budget, and a successful one learns to be flexible as that budget changes on the long road to becoming a viable movie. Budgetary constraints, like any creative constraints, can lead to masterpieces, and even on rare occasions to blockbusters (like *The Blair Witch Project*). A lower budget just tends to "narrow the target," as producers like to say.

If a film is to be made, its budget has to be roughed out before the script ever makes it into the hands of a financier, studio, or movie star's agent. Once that number is determined, the producer can break the budget down into costs—"above the line" (meaning the talent), below the line labor (the crew), equipment, location fees, travel, marketing, and contingency (a small reserve to account for unexpected but inevitable costs). Everything from tax breaks to distribution depends on justifying every line in the budget.

Anyone attaching themselves to a project needs to know what kind of movie it is—its genre and strategy—and that depends on its rough budget. It's a producer's job to make sure the script reflects that—to know that you simply cannot have a CGI spectacular without a star attached and a studio behind the project, just as you can't pay $20 million to an actor starring in a Paul Thomas Anderson film. A screenwriter might know all this, but it's a producer's job to work with her to hit the target, without sacrificing what makes it special in the first place.

Berger's conversation with the screenwriter was supposed to be separate from the "creative pass," but they couldn't help getting into the weeds. Where the screenwriter had pared back, Berger suggested adding something back in; where a character or plot point had been cut, he suggested some narrative shorthand to bridge the gap. Without that kind of attentiveness, careless cuts can lead to plot holes.

"[The writer] was doing the fiscally responsible thing,

which I appreciate," Berger explains. "But I was also empowering him to preserve his priorities. You don't want to be defensive or strip down the movie—you want to find compelling ways through it."

Berger seems constitutionally incapable of leaving a project be when he knows it isn't there yet. Not every producer focuses so intensively on the editing process, and even among deeply involved creative producers there are divisions of labor. On the team of (typically) three or four producers who earn that PGA mark on a film, one might spend more time supervising the set while another hammers out the financing deals and still another focuses on team morale and personnel. Whatever team Berger is on, he tends to be the one mostly deeply in the weeds.

But being an editor-producer is not a purely artistic role. After the filming of a movie is done, Berger likes to put in time in the cutting room, working with the director and editor in pursuit of the best possible movie—and also helping ensure it has its desired impact on an audience.

He is sensitive to the popular notion that a producer undermines the director's artistic vision. "If I'm advocating to tighten a movie, that's never from a crassly commercial point of view," he says, "And, frankly, I resent the accusation. Good producers are filmmakers, too. Most producers I know are wholly invested in making a great film that lives up to the director's vision. That doesn't mean we're always, or even usually, right, but we approach it with honest intent. The good news is that artistic excellence and commercial success are virtually always aligned. A bad movie with the right concept or brand *can* work at the box office. But the better-executed, better-reviewed version always works better."

He offers a rousing defense of not only a producer's role but his motivations. The producer uses his knowledge of the entertainment landscape to ensure that the unwritten rules of the market are followed painlessly enough to give the movie its best shot without compromising its artistry.

"We give everything of ourselves to these movies," he says, "and when a film evokes an emotional response from people, it's a rush. When it provokes debate or changes perspectives or inspires someone, it makes all the hard work worthwhile. When a movie simply disappears or is dismissed, it doesn't diminish our love for the movie, but it stings. At some level, we feel like we've let so many talented people down."

Every producer I talked to would bring up (without naming them for the record) a movie or two that never reached their full potential with an audience. Usually it wasn't mentioned as a personal regret; they'd done everything they could, but for one reason or another—the wrong release date, a stubborn director, studio neglect—it just didn't click. In fact, nothing may have gone wrong at all. It was something more like the law of averages; not every movie finds the audience it deserves.

And the audience is the key. A movie wants—needs—to find its audience. And so the audience must be honored. "That does not mean *pander* or *dumb down*," Berger says. "Audiences are incredibly smart and film-literate. The best way to engage them is to push the boundaries of what they've seen before, while delivering on what you're promising: A horror movie should have scares. A comedy should be funny. A prestige movie should have craft and performances worthy of accolades." This is why every Oscar contender has at least one showstopping monologue that can run in an awards nominee montage. "But in all cases, a movie benefits from being original and ambitious."

Berger has certainly had situations in which that resolve was put under incredible stress—simmering disputes with creators over what the edits have looked like. Both parties, he emphasizes, were fighting for what they felt was the best movie.

This is where his *La La Land* partner Jordan Horowitz's maxim comes into play; the producer's loyalty is not to any particular player or element or financier of the film, but to the film itself. Contractually, Berger often gets final cut of a film, but on principle, he refuses to invoke it. The director always gets final say—though there have been some harrowing impasses.

"There's a moment where it's easier to give up," Berger says. "And you don't get paid more to keep working on a movie. In fact, it's inefficient—it takes time away from building future projects." But he hasn't been able to walk away. "There's a maximum potential for a movie, and, alongside the director, we won't stop until we believe it's hit that ceiling."

Berger isn't shy about his strengths, but he'll readily concede those cases where he was wrong about an edit. The biggest one was *La La Land*.

Many producers rely not just on focus groups but also "friends and family" screenings for savvy guests. It's an important tool and, Berger says, an artistically crucial one. "The lesson I've learned across many movies is that if an audience consistently rejects a certain element, it is typically the case that we will hear the same complaints upon release. If eighty out of one hundred people tell you it's twenty minutes too long, eighty percent of critics and audiences will likely agree."

Sometimes that feedback will cut against the producer's own perspective. "I can't tell you how many times I've been dead wrong about a scene in a movie that I fought for or against, and nothing makes me happier than to learn that with time to fix it. Of course, it's still crucial to protect the core of the film, not to overreact to every note."

When *La La Land* was in postproduction, Berger argued vehemently that Chazelle should cut the opening musical number—an ensemble piece in which drivers stuck in freeway traffic emerge from their cars and sing ironically about love and longing in L.A.

Screenings of an early version received soft marks for the movie's opening—traffic scene included. But when they tested again without the traffic song, the audience was jarred by the second number, which was now the first. "We learned that, for some people, the first musical moment would always be a tough adjustment. But I worried the traffic number in particular could be tonally misleading."

Chazelle instinctively arrived at the exact opposite con-clusion; rather than ease into the number after a prolonged title sequence, he wanted to announce loudly, from the first frame, that you were in for a big, bold musical. He recon-structed the traffic number as a separate prologue, and sud-denly the audience was game. "I was one hundred percent convinced the movie would be released without the traf-fic number," says Berger. "And I was one hundred percent wrong. Thank God Damien didn't listen to me! It doesn't matter whose ideas make it into a movie; the only thing that matters is the film itself."

Whatever you think of *La La Land*, that opening traffic scene is impossible to forget. Did it help the movie become a blockbuster? Perhaps. But it also made it iconic.

ONE OF THE HAZARDS of handling more and bigger pic-tures, as Berger is trying to do, is that your attention is pulled in more directions. You have less time to pore over a budget pass or get through every edit in time for a meet-ing. On the other hand, Berger has spent years becoming more organized, learning to delegate, seeing problems fur-ther ahead and fixing them faster. This is true in any challenging field, but particularly in an industry with so many moving parts.

Berger spends much of the afternoon shifting gears yet again, moving on to a big-budget streaming series barreling toward production—a show whose complex, choose-your-own-adventure structure makes it more intricate to produce, too. He has one conference-room meeting and a couple phone calls about staffing up—conversations that involve everything from checking union rules in different cities to assessing a behind-the-camera talent to figuring out how serious a potential filmmaker is when they tell him they're "seriously" interested in signing on. (In Hollywood, subtext *really* matters.)

Suddenly the day is wrapping up, which is a good thing because it's starting to feel a little like the show Berger's making: a choose-your-own-adventure in which the adventure chooses you, and you just have to ride it out and hope the pieces eventually fit. The only way to wind down from such a day is to get dinner and some drinks at the San Vicente Bungalows.

Are there many professions in which you overcome the stress of a day by going somewhere you're bound to run into the same people you've just been on the phone with? Perhaps a few. It works for Berger—usually.

"It's a common refrain when I talk to students curious about a career in entertainment," he says on the drive over. "If you value work-life balance, I have a lot of industries for you, but this is probably not the one. Family always comes first, but beyond that, this is a twenty-four-seven business, where the line between social and professional is blurred."

What might look superficial on the surface, Berger sees as an incubator of ideas, a palm-fronded courtyard populated by "intelligent, passionate people who are obsessively devoted to the work. The edict is true here: Find something you love and you'll never work a day in your life. Are money, power, celebrity alluring to some people? I'm sure it is. But all of it takes a staggering degree of work and determination."

As soon as we're settled at a table overlooking the patio, passersby start connecting, Berger included. An agent walks by and Berger presses him, jovially, for a yes or no on an actress he's been offering a part. "It's a pass," says the agent. "We should move on." Despite the bad news, Berger seems buoyed. "I love a quick pass," says Berger. "A three-month 'maybe' is brutal." Producing, as many will tell you, is about "hearing no all the time, and sometimes turning nos into yeses." But you have to pick your nos.

In the course of the next two hours our table is joined

by a succession of industry players—a manager colleague; a fellow producer in the trenches; someone who designs a movie's marketing materials. As the population at the table fluctuates between two and six people, conversation meanders across projects, war stories, specific gossip, and general principles. To a passing observer it might feel like a scene from Robert Altman's dark classic *The Player*—sharks trading jibes in overlapping snatches of name-dropping. But from the inside it's just a more festive version of any business convention or office canteen: highs and lows, tricks of the trade, small asks and big ideas. There are also martinis and very good prawns.

One younger producer asks Berger how he handles the calamites of production.

"The disasters are often met with miracles, so you have to work through them," Berger says. Experience is all about learning that everything is survivable. "Early on, every problem feels catastrophic. Yet somehow a solution emerges. You learn that crises are inevitable and there's always a way through. We've never *not* figured it out."

The conversation turns to more specific challenges. What does Berger do, a colleague asks, if an actor offers her own revisions on a script without bringing it to the director?

"Never get between a director and a lead actor," he says. "That's a sacred relationship. You have to help avoid break-downs in communication, but if an actor perceives daylight between the director and producer, that essential trust is broken. You need to get both sides to meet for the film's sake."

He is talking about the on-set dynamics beneath the visible clamor, the side conversations and hidden insecurities the producer must manage, always tending carefully to each participant's basic need. For the director, it's the inviolable sense of being in charge of her own vision. But one manager at the table chimes in to say that actors are the ones with real power: "They're actually the studio."

"I have profound admiration for actors," Berger says. "There's a perception that they have it easy. You'd be amazed by the amount of work and pressure they take on, and they are by far the most *exposed*. Their face is literally front and center. It's a trust fall. In the edit, we have the power to massage a rocky performance, but also the capacity to undermine stellar work. I could never handle the lack of control. Luckily, I'm an abysmal actor!"

The marketing executive who's come by the table is naturally more interested in the later phases of moviemaking.

His job begins when the editing is done. He handles the aesthetic dimension of the message that brings the movie to public awareness—trailers, posters, billboards, film titles, supplemental press kits. Not that the producer's job ends there. "The reason you're so valuable," Berger tells him, "is that our work doesn't stop when a movie's finished. If we're not hyper-vigilant about the release date and marketing, a great movie can die."

During Berger's time in the producing wilderness—those seven years between credits—he had an unusual hobby; he was in a "fantasy movie league." He and some industry friends, including Horowitz, would handicap forthcoming films based on their marketing and rollouts, trying to game out their trajectory and ultimate success or failure. "I became academic about release dates and strategies," Berger says. "I realized how much certain people who hold the levers of power don't understand that a specialized movie needs a bespoke path."

Berger brings up two specific movies, similarly sized releases from the same company, that fared differently because one opened on the same weekend as a major franchise film, while the other found a less competitive niche. One of Berger's great struggles has been to lobby for the right release date in the right amount of theaters, in order to boost on-screen averages and avoid burying a movie on the wrong weekend. The most successful strategy for a smaller prestige movie is usually to build an audience gradually through word of mouth and positive press, not to bombard them on day one.

We're about to leave when an agent wanders over. He and Berger catch up on their families before talking more generally about producers. The agent quotes a veteran in his field: "He told me, 'There are a lot of great directors, great actors, great writers. The hardest thing to do is find a great producer.' It's a jack-of-all-trades, but at the same time, you have to have the most specific skills."

Berger wonders whether the producer's value is recognized enough outside the industry—whether it's the kind of job people feel motivated to pursue.

"But Fred," the agent says, "for the people who are in it, there's no question of value. If you're actually in it, you know exactly how important that job is."

Berger thanks him, and then gently brings up another matter. "I'm looking for directors on two projects," he says. "Should I talk to you about it?" And with that, it's back to work.

The next morning in the office, Berger reports that he'd gone home and stayed up watching *The Talented Mr. Ripley* before bed. ("Still holds up.") But he seems to have shaken off the late night. The day fills up with details of postproduction on projects on the smaller side. On one film, a late change requested by a top talent has forced Berger to go back to a major investor and then the investor's attorney—a pair of uncomfortable but necessary calls. For the film it might be the difference between glory and obscurity, so he does what he has to do, tries to turn a no into a yes.

There's another smaller movie for which Berger has high hopes, another source of frustration today. This one is nearly finished, headed—he hopes—for major festivals, but right now it needs to appeal to distributors. Indie movies often sell to foreign markets on the strength of a promo, a long-form ad giving a little more mood and plot than a standard trailer. But on a morning call with the movie's two sales agents, everyone agrees that the latest pass of the promo still isn't delivering. It's true—Berger later shows me the promo cut, which is vague and tonally inconsistent.

"Version two is better than version one, but we need to keep working on it," Berger says. "This promo needs to knock you out or it's not gonna move the needle. I'm happy to keep working on it—I'll roll up my sleeves and dive in, but the trailer house," the company devoted to making film trailers, "needs to be in the trenches with me for the next two weeks."

Berger and the agents hop on a phone call with the trailer house and Berger delivers the news as gently as he can. "Great leap forward," he says. "We're all encouraged with the progress. However, we're still not feeling that this piece will fully motivate people to buy it." He asks for specific clips, mentions missing beats.

A half dozen scattered calls later, Berger checks in with me and flashes a broad smile. It seems the day has ended with a small win, but a win nonetheless. It was about the musical project he had co-pitched at 8 a.m. the previous morning, nervous and groggy, in which he'd appealed to the emotional power of the underdog story.

Based on notes in the thirty-six hours since, he wasn't sure the company was ready to fund development, but finally, at the end of this day, they had called for some reassurance. Again, he pushed the comparison to other quirky but successful movies. It was Gus Van Sant, but *Good Will Hunting* Gus Van Sant, not *Elephant* Gus Van Sant. By the end of the call, he felt good about it. "I got an email earlier that was feeling like a no, and now it's feeling like a yes."

A FEW WEEKS LATER, Berger is in New York doing staffing prep for the choose-your-own-adventure series. I catch him once again at the Bowery Hotel, between meetings with writers. Berger has something to show me, but first, he runs down a few updates.

The high-profile biopic is coming together, with details of the director's contract still being ironed out. The investor on the movie with last-minute expenses didn't come through with the extra cash, but he found another source of funding. The sci-fi script has moved into its creative pass, though the budget is still in flux, and may expand again.

But Berger has still got that promotional trailer on his mind. "A trailer should always be better than the movie," he says. "You take all the best material, put it to great music, and compress it to two minutes—there's no excuse." Berger generally swears by one trailer shop, Mark Woollen, often recognized as the best in the prestige corner of the business (*Birdman*; *The Social Network*; *La La Land*). But this particular movie had already hired a European house via their sales company.

A couple weeks ago, Berger had gone on a run and thought through every shot, then gotten home and scribbled down his thoughts before they evaporated. Working with the trailer editors, over several more versions, they have arrived at a new cut—he has it on his phone right now and is excited to show me the progress. It does look a lot better: clearer exposition, flashy moments, a sense of the story, and a few emotional gut punches. It's a movie you'd want to see.

He seems both proud and a little bit frustrated with the detailed work involved, work that took time away from bigger-picture planning. "A lot of what I want the next phase of my career to be is getting a little less in the weeds on the minutiae." A bigger-budget picture, backed by a studio or platform with deep resources, would allow him to delegate more day-to-day tasks. There'd be fewer individual investors to court, less cajoling of distributors, less concern over threading the needle of improbable success. But when I ask which phase of production he'd like to outsource first, he hesitates.

"Part of what I love about producing is you have to be a jack-of-all-trades," he says. "It's the ideal left-brain, right-brain job—you get to be an artist, a storyteller, a lawyer, a politician, an editor, a therapist, and most importantly, you're always learning. I'm just beginning to feel that I'm not completely faking it anymore." He notes that his first production company, with Garcia, was literally called Impostor Pictures. "That's what I love most about the job. Each project has its own challenges and joys, and that unscalable mountain keeps it energizing." Passing off responsibility seems like a trade he doesn't want to master just yet.

5

THE ADAPTER

The contrast between Automatik's sleek surfaces and the office suite of Groundswell, Michael London's outfit on Wilshire Boulevard, is fairly striking. Groundswell has a small corner kitchen with a coffee maker. The ceiling is paneled and there's a glass-walled conference room and a central area no different from that of, say, a small literary agency—gray carpeting, three desks, scattered papers.

London's spacious office, where most meetings take place, is much more stylish and personalized—decked out with posters and prizes from movies that hit the sweet spot of indie film success: *Milk*, *Sideways*, *Trumbo*, *Thirteen*. The wall-to-wall view of the Los Angeles Basin unfurling itself into the Pacific is spectacular and gauzy. Yet Groundswell's overhead is modest, its lavishness well-curated. It's a place that knows itself, knows where it stands, even as its employees scramble every day to find purchase for its brand of accessible prestige. There's room for that somewhere in the industry, but the niche is a moving target. London's job is to find it and pin it down long enough to put an idea on screen.

During the two days I visited Groundswell, it was quieter than Automatik, but just as intensely consumed with potential projects. This particular week, London has a bad cold, so he only comes in for a handful of long meetings and takes the rest of his calls at home—all mediated from the office desk of Sarah Freedman, the former New Yorker who had the tough experience at WME. Jordan Mahoney, meanwhile, handles the calls of Shannon Gaulding, Michael's recently arrived executive and number two. Freedman and Mahoney, having found their way from the Weinstein Company, seem relieved by the change of atmosphere.

London's first meeting of the day is with a screenwriter he's known for years, but only seen on rare occasions. They started out with similar tastes and aspirations, but both have gone their own ways; the writer found security in a giant action franchise, a perpetual sequel machine that's been going for years, under the radar of many American viewers, but it's currently buoyed by the Chinese market (in both audience and financing). He's been hoping to buy time to pursue more meaningful work—the kind he wants to talk to London about. "The hassle with my part of the job," says the writer, "is that I have to spend so much time chasing a paying gig that it keeps me from doing the passion projects."

They begin by talking about their families, then try to remember the occasion for their last meeting. That's when the writer points to London's coffee table. "I think I came to talk to you, for whatever reason, about that." On the table is a hardcover copy of *A Visit from the Goon Squad*, Jennifer Egan's Pulitzer Prize–winning episodic novel of various intersecting characters in the worlds of art, music, and fashion, the timeline running from the 1970s to a strange near-future New York. In other words, perfect for a TV series. London has been trying to get it made for years. Like Berger, he is necessarily fatalistic and constitutionally optimistic.

London says it's been through four networks and come close to production several times. There's a new network trying to help make it right now. "We're running into the same problem that everybody has always had with it," he says. "They are afraid it is too literary, which ignores the fact that the book is set in the music world and touches on universal themes. They want a big star. It's an obsession of mine because of my own musical past. I pray that maybe this is the moment it happens."

"Why is it so fucking difficult," says the writer, more in sorrow than in anger.

London's enthusiasm doesn't flag. "We have two episodes, some of the best scripts I've ever worked on." It's not the first or last time London brings up a project he is certain will get made, if not this year then maybe the next, or five years from now. "It's extraordinary material," he says. "It's just that with this kind of project all the stars have to align. And the television marketplace is shifting away from material like this."

The marketplace has been shifting ever since London first got to know it in the '80s. His career is instructive in two ways: first as the journey of a producer trying every path before finding the right one, and second as the story of an industry subject to multiple waves of seismic change. As a producer London has moved from accidental executive to independent striver, then investor-backed financier-CEO, and finally an arty producer with powerful commercial alliances.

These personal shifts were also adaptations to Hollywood, an ecosystem beset by environmental shocks. After independent movies blossomed in the '90s, Berger's fabled time of mid-budget indie masterpieces, they attracted money from Wall Street, then withered as the Great Recession hit and the studios became interested only in sure-fire franchises. Fortunately, this creative drought gave way to a second golden age of prestige—only this time on TV (both cable and streaming). Today, the television pendulum is swinging back to the commercial, as everyone from HBO to ABC expands subscription services by catering again to "four-quadrant TV," meaning shows for the masses. (Each "quadrant" represents a demographic: male under twenty-five, female under twenty-five, male over twenty-five, female over twenty-five.) An ecosystem that changes this rapidly not only rewards adaptation but demands it, even at the highest level of artistry.

Like Lynda Obst, who moved out West from a New York job as a magazine editor, London began as a journalist. But his path was even more unusual and circuitous than hers. Raised in Minneapolis, London went to Stanford and graduated with no intention of going into film. He got an internship with the entertainment section of the *Los Angeles Times* and quickly began writing for them. His passion, which he still pursues today as a producer, was rock music.

One of his first stories was about the US Festival, a sort of early-'80s proto-Coachella. The assignment was a disaster, with most journalists consigned to a remote "island" where they were unable to even see the bands. "I wrote this tongue-in-cheek story: 'I covered the US Festival without ever seeing the music.' " He was into X and the Blasters, the late L.A. punks. He's always wanted to make a movie about the Sex Pistols' ill-fated tour of America from a journalist's point of view, a grittier version of *Almost Famous*.

London's big break came, most unexpectedly, after he profiled two filmmakers and fellow Minnesotans. ("Midnight has struck in a small rented house atop the hills of Silver Lake, and the Coen brothers of Minneapolis are Trying to Explain It.") His piece about the auteur wunderkinds caught the attention of Don Simpson, who—with producing partner Jerry Bruckheimer—had made *Flashdance*, *Beverly Hills Cop*, *Top Gun*, and *The Rock*, among other generation-defining hits. "Don loved the idea of hiring people who were outsiders," and he and Bruckheimer asked London to work for him. London resisted the offer; he just didn't see himself working in the entertainment business. But he was ambivalent about journalism and agreed to take a flier for a year.

The industry grew on him: "I became enamored of the more creative side of the business. Getting to do storytelling in film was exciting." But Simpson-Bruckheimer wasn't a perfect fit creatively. After two years, he made a connection at Fox and took an executive job. "I went from working for two ultra-commercial producers to being a corporate executive, which was another job I wasn't exactly well-suited to—but I did better at that one, and I learned a lot."

There are plenty of people more suited to executive jobs than independent production. It's a steadier and usually bigger paycheck; it affords you the opportunity to think bigger picture about the year's slate of films; it's just as hard-charging but more routinized. You can have a family without dragging them off to set every six months. You have an army of assistants helping you and the power of an institution behind your decisions. At the same time, you are beholden to the priorities of the people you work for.

"It very much depends on who you are," says Obst, "but I would not want to be an executive. I like my creative freedom and I like to buy whatever film I want. I don't want to be on the agenda for the corporation."

London put in five years for Fox, until he realized "I was swimming upstream. So I went on my own as a producer and that's when it really clicked for me. I knew a lot of writers from my time with Simpson-Bruckheimer and Fox and those relationships gave me a head start." He also retained an important connection with Fox; he was a producer with a deal on the Fox lot.

It's a comfortable position for many, if you can get it. Obst has a deal with Sony to this day. They pay for her office and assistants. "You're a supplier for them," she says. "Your job is to move your material toward what they're looking for. That's the advantage and disadvantage. But you're not an employee." If something doesn't work for them and Obst likes it enough, she can shop it around wherever she likes.

But for London, this middle ground between studio executive and truly independent producer still wasn't enough; his tastes were too specific—not too small, just too risky. "It was the first time I felt unsuccessful at what I was doing," he says. "The problem wasn't the job, it was that, as a producer on a studio lot, you're still looking for the same commercial projects that an executive is supposed to find. The jobs really aren't that different since the movies are the same."

Today, the distinction might be moot for a younger producer; London's path might not even be feasible. Over the last decade the number of producer deals has dropped precipitously—a consequence of the shrinking slates of most studios and belt-tightening on overhead. Shannon Gaulding, the newish executive at Groundswell, spent eleven years on the Sony studio lot—almost nine of those at Columbia Pictures. "I think they had forty-five deals [with producers], and now they have about four," she says. "You had somebody paying for your rent and your phones and you had a decent copier down the hall and maybe you had an assistant."

But for London, it was as difficult an untethering as Berger's premature break with Ross Katz: "I left the lot, and I was a little lost," he says. "I left my relatively plush job and office and assistant and I was working out of my house, and I was fairly newly married and it caused us a great deal of anxiety. Financially, it was a big risk." He carved out a second-bedroom office space and went scrounging for scripts. He even wrote one, which he sold. "But I just knew from reading great screenplays that I couldn't write to that level," he says. "As a producer, I wasn't impressed enough with what the writer was doing."

His first success was critically acclaimed but financially unrewarding: Catherine Hardwicke's *Thirteen*, a groundbreaking coming-of-age movie that presaged a big-budget career (including *Twilight*). He deferred his fee for the experience of making something he loved. It was a crucial first step in gaining acclaim and building relationships with artists; when we met, he was developing two separate TV projects with Hardwicke all these years later. But at the time it wasn't enough to get London off the runway. It took another project to do that.

"Rex Pickett, an indie writer and director whom I met when I first moved to Los Angeles, was working on an auto-biographical first novel called 'Two Guys on Wine.' " It was about two men driving through California's wine country on an epic tasting bender, eventually coming to terms with their demons and nurturing their souls in the same hardy soil that breeds an exquisite pinot noir.

London believed the manuscript could make a great film, and he thought it should be directed by the up-and-coming filmmaker Alexander Payne. The fellow Stanford grad had gotten a lot of attention for *Citizen Ruth*, starring Laura Dern. London went to Sundance in 1996, the year of that movie's premiere, stood in line to shake Payne's hand, and thought, *Someday I'm going to call him up and have something great to share with him.*

By the time Pickett's novel was ready, Payne had made *Election*—the kind of breakthrough success that can make a filmmaker much harder to get on the phone. London went through the proper channels, sent Payne the script, and heard nothing back for months—until one Friday night. As he remembers it, he was just about ready to call an end to his indie producing adventure. "I had decided that the following Monday morning I was going to start looking for a job," he says. "I couldn't maintain this quixotic desire to be an independent producer."

But around 7 p.m. that Friday, the phone rang in London's home office, and he reached it on the eleventh ring. It was Payne. He said, "This is Alexander Payne and I'd be honored to make this wonderful book into a movie." This being real life, however, it wasn't so simple. Two months later, Payne called to say that he was on the hook to make a bigger movie immediately. He asked if London and Pickett were willing to wait while he made the big-studio Jack Nicholson vehicle *About Schmidt*.

They agreed. "It was very painful and at many points it seemed like a mistake, because the stories of directors who change their minds are legion." But sometimes a producer has to hold out hope for the perfect pairing of director and film. A year later, Payne invited London to a screening of a rough cut of *About Schmidt*.

"There was a scene where Nicholson's character was riding his camper through an old dusty town, and there was an old movie theater, and on the marquee it said, 'COMING SOON: SIDEWAYS.' It was a private message in his $25 million Sony movie, basically saying, 'I'm not going to let you down.' "

The writing process was smooth, but casting took time.

The project came to the inevitable crossroads: Did it need big stars to justify its budget? For a moment George Clooney and Brad Pitt were pursuing the roles of (respectively) the curmudgeon and the B-movie actor galoot.

But Payne wanted run-of-the-mill guys, and he wouldn't budge. His everyman wasn't Clooney but Paul Giamatti, and his out-of-work actor had to be played by someone with a similar trajectory. London told Payne that he would have to cut the budget by at least a third in order to have his preferred cast. "Alexander said, 'I'd rather make the movie for $10 or $11 million with unknowns than a $17 million movie with stars.' "

Add it to the list of cases in which a producer was happy to have been wrong. Fox Searchlight improbably approved the $17 million budget, and the movie made more than $100 million worldwide.

At the time, there were many movies made at that budget level; you've never heard of most of them. A movie that has staying power is usually one that also far exceeded its budget expectations. (And it's that ratio, more than raw box-office numbers, that really matters.) For a producer on the rise, cultural influence is a huge motivator, but—barring some long-tail cult hit—that's impossible without reaching a larger-than-expected audience. The producer is responsible for that success. Often, it's enough to make a career; invariably, it's a perpetual calling card.

On the strength of *Sideways* and two other successful projects, *The Family Stone* and *The Illusionist*, London had enough to set himself up. "I was riding the tail end of the indie movie explosion. There was a lot of excitement about the notion that you could find broader audiences for more personal films." These were hardly avant-garde, but they occupied a space for character-driven wide-release movies that was as large as it had ever been—and possibly ever would be.

In 2006, Groundswell was born, the fruit of a collaboration with CAA (Creative Artists Agency) and a number of capital investors from Wall Street. The financial boom of the late aughts lifted all boats, even indie films. London hired about a dozen people, including a couple of executives. The company made *Milk*, *The Mysteries of Pittsburgh*, and *The Informant!*, among others. And then the bottom fell out.

Two giant markets collapsed simultaneously in 2008— the one for stocks and the one for DVDs. The first crash cut right into the heart of London's financing, while the second emptied out a major source of customer revenue. DVD sales were crucial to the indie movie boom. A DVD deal could account for a third of the money recouped in distribution sales—as much as a domestic theatrical release. When that revenue stream went away, so did a lot of movies without initial studio backing.

Between those two forces, London lost his funding and had to return to the life of an independent producer. Today, he looks back on those flush years as "a mixed experience. I loved the producing but managing a big group of people didn't play to my strengths." The duties of a CEO just didn't suit him. He had tried being an executive before and realized producing was a better fit; now he wanted to go back to it. In any event, he didn't have a choice. "I had to regather myself a second time and move on."

Helping his transition was his ownership stake in the company's films—an unusual arrangement for a producer that London managed only because he was also financing movies, backed by Wall Street investors. This gave him a significant cushion while heading back out on his own.

The way out of his producing impasse is obvious if you've been watching anything over the past decade. Even before the model for indie film production began to buckle, TV—the erstwhile province of the lowbrow—had begun to rise in prestige. HBO and other cable channels began running TV-as-art, setting off a competitive market that flourished and spawned more and more conversation-piece shows. Eventually we reached "Peak TV," the modern age in which it's impossible to keep up with every show critics are talking about. Early on in that arc, it became clear to London that survival in quality screen projects meant becoming a television producer. For all the hard adjustments to a serial format and a Silicon Valley–dominated market, it felt like a fair trade, and still does. London got to produce one of Amazon's very first shows, *Betas*, back when it wasn't much like a studio at all.

"It reminded me of *Sideways* and *Thirteen*," he says, "where the financiers said, 'Go off and make what you want to make.' People just wanted to hire talented filmmakers. No one calls the shots when they make movies with Alexander Payne, and I was never interested in movies where I was calling the shots." He also went back to a first-look deal, a sort of scaled down studio deal, with a television arm of Fox.

London rode the content boom with projects generally in keeping with his taste; when he delved into genre—a staple of television even more than film—there was always a strong storytelling element. For FX, he made *Snowfall*, a *Wire*-like series on the crack epidemic in '80s L.A.; for Showtime, he made *SMILF*, a dark, raunchy comedy about a single mother; *The Magicians*, adapted from a literary fantasy series by Lev Grossman, was wrapping its fifth and final season for SyFy when I visited London.

"I got to be there for a second golden moment," says London, before lamenting—as many do—the latest bump in the road: the rush of legacy companies into platforms like Disney+, Peacock, and CBSNow, studios that forced the tech innovators to start acting more like studios.

"There's no way to rail against that," he says. "And television is so huge now that you can find these little niches where, if you're in the right place at the right time, you can get something really interesting done."

ASIDE FROM LONDON'S ONE-on-one with the screenwriter, every meeting I witness that day at Groundswell involves all four full-time employees: London; Freedman, the assistant; Mahoney, director of development; and Gaulding, the new exec. (London's producing partner for eleven years, Janice Williams, left the company in 2018.) The linchpin of the day is a rapid-fire status-update meeting, running through twenty projects in an hour. The cumulative effect of watching it brings home one of Mahoney's earlier metaphors about a producer's job: moving multiple boulders up a hill.

They run through a graphic novel series being eyed for production by a Canadian broadcaster (a solid source of tax breaks), followed by a summary of reviews for a small movie that was struggling at the box office. "They're totally right," says London, as the group coos sympathetically. "Great subject matter, great story, but it may have been too bleak for a broad audience."

They move on quickly. "Okay, *Magicians* wrap party, I may go up for that," says London. The show is done shooting its fifth season, and the producer should be there to celebrate in Vancouver. "*Snowfall*," he says, turning to Gaulding and Mahoney. "So I don't know how engaged you want to be with this. The room just started; the writers' notes are coming out. I'd love to have one of you engaged."

Mahoney volunteers. The writers' room on the show is just starting to set down season four; at this stage of a show's run, a producer's engagement is optional. One advantage of a longer-running series is that it becomes a machine long after the producer's heavy lifting is done. "You can still be involved," London says, "but you don't have to. No one's looking at you to put out fires." Financially, it nets an annual fee equivalent to that of a small indie film—a steady source of income and a boulder rolling forward, subsidizing all the Sisyphean struggles that end in repeated failure.

Speaking of which, next on the list is a movie that feels tantalizingly close and yet nowhere near getting made. Based on a bestselling novel, the multigenerational epic has a director attached who is best known for a blockbuster franchise. It's a major opportunity, but it means working with a filmmaker accustomed to "unlimited means" who insists on a $40 million budget—a step down for him, but a number that London's producing partners can't justify, despite the talent, which includes a legendary older actress. "They're running the numbers again," London reports, hoping against hope that a gap of millions of dollars can be bridged. "No one wants to move," he says with a sigh. They might have to lose the director in order to make a lower-budget version.

The team moves to TV. They recap a meeting from earlier in the day with the writer on a project based on a YA fantasy series. They had spent an hour getting into the weeds—with Gaulding going deepest—not just honing a presentation to shop around to networks but poking at the underlying story, trying to help drive the plot forward.

"It would be nice to have the author pitching with us," London had said at the earlier meeting. "She's such a fun presence." The author was the reason the story was viable as a show, possessing a rabid fan base built at fan conventions partly on the strength of her charisma. Gaulding would be introducing the project and the writer would be doing the overview of the season—leaving out just enough to hint that there was a bottomless well of material left over for subsequent seasons.

"I'm feeling really good about the character stuff," Gaulding had said. "I'm really good on the pilot stuff, although I think it's running a little long. It needs a little editing." They proceeded to talk about character motivation—"running toward something and not away from something."

Groundswell is collaborating on the show with Legendary Pictures, a genre-focused production outfit with which they have a first-look deal on genre material. Instead of the old model of a producer linked up with a single mega-studio, adaptive indie producers like London might make deals involving niches, catering to a system much more fragmented than it was in the oligarchic heyday of one-stop shops like Sony and Paramount. It's more like a partnership, in which the two linked companies pitch to the platforms and some of those very same studios, teaming up and leveraging their collective power to get a show made and seen. In return, Legendary helps with Groundswell's overhead costs.

This particular project is hardly a slam dunk. In fact, it will end up being frozen in the development stage, as it turns out the writer is working on a new offshoot of the series with potentially broader appeal. But in these early days, you can see why it has a good shot. Like *Magicians*, it's a genre project with a built-in audience and seasons full of plots contained in the books. In the era of streaming shows and "tentpole" movies whose box office pays for the whole year, IP (adapted material) is king.

But in the meantime it's a labor of love for Gaulding, who loves to dig into the details of whatever she happens to be working on. After she left Columbia, Gaulding worked for another Sony division called Screen Gems, known for the *Underworld* and *Resident Evil* franchises, but she stuck to more middle-of-the-road pictures like *Dear John*, starring Channing Tatum, that did well. Then she went to an outfit called Hollywood Gang, which made its name and its money on the movie *300*. But that company's work has been shifting overseas, according to Gaulding, so she's come over to Groundswell, bearing an armful of leftover projects while helping with London's workload.

She makes a few calls while I'm in the office, mostly managing two incipient projects. One is starring an actor who had a huge role on a premium-cable blockbuster—despite which she's having trouble cobbling together enough money to get the movie made. "It's a Western, which is a nightmare," she says. "We got turned down a lot of places. Even though he's a big TV star, the international market is still driven by old white guys—think Nic Cage. With TV there's no box-office numbers for foreign distributors to pull." For all the fluidity between TV and film, some elements don't translate, at least where financing is concerned.

The other film Gaulding is dealing with is much smaller, a documentary about Choctaw stickball—a traditional game that modern Native Americans in the Deep South still play as they try to balance expressions of their heritage with the modern challenges of life on the reservation. The movie has to be restructured because the original narrative just wasn't cohering; documentaries are shot without a script, creating challenges in postproduction. Gaulding is pushing to accelerate the post schedule so they have a shot at a Sundance slot. (The festival will occur in late January and it's now late October.) "If we don't get in, we can slow down," she says. "But we have to go until we know."

Back at the status meeting, the team discusses another potential book adaptation, and the team's frustration over the relentless churn of making calls and waiting for answers bubbles over. London is going out to Alexander Payne to direct, but that's not the issue; it's getting one studio considering the project to answer the phone—if only to pass so they can move on.

"I went to lunch with them on Tuesday and I was going to ping them softly today," says Gaulding. "[A development VP] sent an email looping in [her boss], and she didn't have it yet."

"How hard is it to get an outline from somebody else in your department?" says London.

"It took her two days to email the person who sits next to her," says Gaulding. "So I think what I'll probably do is email them again tomorrow."

"But they're not gonna say anything until [the head of television] has read it, and he's not gonna read it until the weekend." As with so many of Berger's calls, it takes experience to know who's serious and who isn't, and who's actually making the decisions.

Other projects are even more dependent on the whims of the industry. Take the next item on the agenda, *Whistleblower*, a project of Gaulding's that was built as an anthology series, in which each season is a separate story. The show would spend the first season on the story of a particular truth-teller, Karen Silkwood, the nuclear-plant whistleblower (played by Meryl Streep in *Silkwood*) who was killed in 1974 on the way to a meeting with the *New York Times*, files full of damning evidence in her possession.

"Anthology's so hard," Gaulding sighs. "We sold the show to FX and now, with the Disney sale, FX has dumped a lot of projects at once; all their old development is out. And when we took it back out again there were a few places that passed, straight-up refusing to even read the script: 'We're just not doing anthologies.' "

A few years ago, at the height of the hype over Ryan Murphy's shows (*Feud, American Horror Story*), anthology series looked like the unstoppable wave of the future. But by 2019, the format had gone out of vogue. Trends are an occupational hazard in Hollywood, of course, but in London's office it feels dismaying that the barrier to turning fantastic concepts into filmed reality isn't an outmoded subject or the lack of a star, but a story structure that may have missed its moment by three short years.

Finally, we get to a show on which all the pieces seem to be falling into place. "*Yellow Bird*," London announces. "Sterlin spoke to Lissa this morning, said it went really well. So she's going on a hunt in Oklahoma and he lives in Oklahoma . . ."

Yellow Bird, if and when it gets made, will be an archetypal Michael London production, in that it will bear no particular stamp of his. He is, paradoxically, the kind of producer who takes his greatest pride in those projects where, as he said of a Payne movie, "no one calls the shots" but the artists who make them. *Yellow Bird*, at the time of this meeting, is a still-unpublished book: an intensely immersive nonfiction story by journalist Sierra Crane Murdoch about a Native American woman, Lissa Yellow Bird, living on a North Dakota reservation who uncovers a murder conspiracy and becomes an amateur sleuth despite having a checkered past of her own.

"I just fell in love with it," London told me a couple months before the status meeting. "It's the most powerful book I've read in many years."

When you read about a book that's been sold or optioned, there's always a producer behind it—even if the name in the headline is Sony or Netflix. Producers will rarely buy books outright; they usually purchase the rights to develop it into a script, gather talent around the project, and shop it around for a set period, normally eighteen months. These days, when the hunger for IP is limitless, competition for books can be fierce well before their publication date. Literary agents specializing in film rights will slip manuscripts to scouts, who will meet with producers like London or development execs like Mahoney. The first one to spot the talent and come up with the right concept—and charm the author—will get the deal.

Getting Murdoch's sign-off on the option wasn't so difficult for London—they bonded over another London passion project, Adrian Nicole LeBlanc's bestselling and critically acclaimed book *Random Family*. But the person he really needed to woo was the owner of the story, Lissa Yellow Bird.

London's next call was to the Sundance Producing Labs, which has a department exclusively focused on Native American stories. (The same group that will decide if Gaulding's Choctaw stickball documentary gets a festival slot.) One writer came up again and again in London's research: Sterlin Harjo. When London called Harjo's manager, the manager said, "I know why you're calling—because Sterlin's going to be in Vancouver next week." He didn't know what the manager was talking about, but it turned out that Harjo was about to direct an episode of *Magicians*. It felt like serendipity—and a perfect way in.

Harjo not only knew the story of Lissa Yellow Bird but he wanted to tell it. There was, however, one problem: He was already working on a defining Native film, an adaptation of Tommy Orange's novel *There There*. "So I thought, 'Okay, I'm doubly screwed.'" Here was a competing project that also took his best potential writer out of circulation. But in this case, the vicissitudes of Hollywood production worked in London's favor. *There There* seemed to have lost steam in a management changeover, and suddenly Harjo was available.

Now London had to get Lissa Yellow Bird's sign-off. He had the journalist interested, and he had a Native writer excited to do the script. But Yellow Bird had already turned down several producers. London thought he had a trump card, which was actually born of market constraints: it had to be a TV show. "Ten years ago," he says, "it would have been a movie and I would have been excited about it as a movie. But as a series it's possible to tell a much broader story that will include Lissa as well as her family members and members of her community." Across multiple seasons he could unfurl the context that had made the book so rich: Lissa's relationship to the land, her family, and the region's long history of exploitation by white people hungry for their oil. "Who wouldn't want to do that?"

But the approach had to be delicate; he was willing to go to North Dakota, to meet Yellow Bird on her turf and explain that he wanted to shoot the show with unknown Native actors—definitely a prerequisite in this era, in which cross-racial casting is a no-no. This meant, of course, that it would be a harder pitch to Hollywood, which was why all the pieces had to align just so. He would need to hire a seasoned and trusted showrunner, someone to oversee the entire series. He was thinking about Susannah Grant. She had worked with him on the HBO movie *Confirmation*, but her credits also include *Party of Five* and the 2019 show *Unbelievable*. She might be too busy to commit, but London assured Grant that her role wouldn't require any heavy lifting until the project was further down the line.

Today at the Groundswell status meeting, London is happy to report that Harjo is going to break bread with Yellow Bird in Oklahoma. "He feels like once he sits down with her it's all done," London says.

Several agenda items later, the team gets to a pair of more speculative projects, both of which will require a lot more research. One is the idea to tell the rich history behind the Mughal Empire and the construction of the Taj Mahal, based on a script that came free of a studio but needs a rewrite. They have a list of books to get through, but Freedman says none of them are available online.

"Can I make a somewhat lame suggestion?" says Gaulding. "Do you have a library card?"

They'll access some of the books overnight and read

them and decide, months later, to base the story on one of those books. But for now, they just have a lot of homework.

Next—and last for the day—is another project that requires a lot of homework. Groundswell has partnered with a streamer to remake an American literary classic—a book that's been adapted into a couple of films.

I ask what the new angle is.

"There is no angle," London says, and everyone laughs. "No, the angle is that it's a limited series where you can do the book justice, as opposed to the movies, which are always these highly condensed, shallow things."

But in order for that to work, they need a writer who can make an impact—someone who is either enormously famous, top-tier but unexpected, or lesser known but brilliant. It's a tall order.

"So we've been going out to namey-names," says Gaulding. They tried *Mad Men* auteur Matt Weiner, but he passed.

"Do they have to showrun?" asks Freedman.

"No," says London, "but better if they do. Okay, so we're really gonna bear down. I may dig into my big writing list."

"And we'll look at some of our more literary project list," says Mahoney.

"Didn't we make a huge master list?" asks Freedman. "I

sent you that whole binder." With that, the meeting breaks up so London can take a phone call—an executive calling back to make a deal on another show. After the call, London delivers the happy news that the deal is ready for the lawyers. Everyone sounds celebratory, relieved.

"Well, that was nice," says Gaulding.

"It *was* nice," says London. "Although it was a bit strange because he said, 'I'm really going to fight hard for this one once we have a script.' And not, 'The company's really excited about it.'" Ultimately, it won't get made.

THE NEXT DAY, FRIDAY, is devoted mostly to tying up loose ends, divvying up the long list of scripts and books to read over the weekend, and digging into that binder of writers, ranging from the famous to the obscure, who might adapt the literary classic for television.

There's a clumsy dance of figuring out which is the correct list to print out; because London had already skipped over so many names they now have to go back to, it's not immediately discernible which writers he wants to rescue from the swipe-left pile. Once they sort that out, they run through the list and then add more, and more, and more.

The point is to comb through every possibility, discuss their suitability and—just as important—availability. Some of the best-known writers have "overalls," exclusive deals with studios. Groundswell already has a distribution partner on this project, so that won't work. (This is a powerful limitation on the pool of talent London can use on every picture he makes; if he wants a writer with an overall, he has to go with their studio, which could be wrong for the project or not interested.)

They go through name after name, some batched together as short lists sent by agencies, others linked merely by associative thinking. There are the reaches with huge shows ("I'm sure she's not available until the end of time"). There are second looks at the previously sidelined ("What's wrong with the Safdie brothers?" London wants them for another show).

There are also writers beloved of one member of the group (not including London, who is working from home). Talk of the writers gets muddled with a more general discussion of shows that Freedman or Mahoney or Gaulding happens to be in love with at the moment. There is Martin McDonagh, Luca Guadagnino, Damien Chazelle. There are lesser-known names that "could be sweet" or "would be really dark" or, come to think of it, are "too blue-collar."

Along the way, they check in on IMDbPro and trade paper headlines to see if the writers are engaged in another project or tied down by a deal. "All right guys, keep them coming," says Gaulding forty minutes into the meeting.

"I'm done, I'm squeezed out," says Freedman.

"Who wrote *Jackie*?" asks Mahoney.

Freedman does manage quite a few more names, and they end up discussing at least seventy in the course of an hour. Gaulding says that her executive years have prepared her for this.

"There's a thousand variations of every list," she says. "This is the training you get at the studio. You crank out lists. I had seven open writing assignments at once and that's all I did for a whole year. It was literally *No Exit*. But it's the underpinning of everything, even if the hunt feels fruitless at times."

In fact, this kind of very purposeful digging can, strangely, lead to happy accidents. "Generally, a lot of it's just conversation starters, things to think about," says Freedman.

"And you'll call an agent," says Mahoney, "and they'll say no, but how about this person? They happen to love [the literary classic].' And a lot of times it comes out of left field."

That's ultimately what almost happened in this one—

another instance of serendipity followed by bad luck, triumph shadowed by defeat, and, ultimately, renewed hope. London had reached out to the agent of one suggested writer, a big hitmaker. He wasn't interested, but the agent knew a legendary playwright who was—who, in fact, had original editions of the classic book. This playwright was very interested, for a long time, and all set to start the development process—until a play of his ran into trouble, and he was rendered unavailable for months. Then it was back to square one.

"It's a little disappointing because I had multiple conversations with him that were really exciting," London reports a few weeks later. "But in another way, it validates the possibility that a great writer will want to do that." If you want to be a producer, you have to find the hopeful message—the push forward—in every missed opportunity. In every haystack, you have to find a needle. And in every "no," you have to find the kernel of a "yes."

6

A VERY WEIRD YEAR

There is no greater gathering place for the collective hopes and dreams of filmmakers—and producers— than one of the hundreds of film festivals scattered across the world, many of them focused on finished movies in search of distribution. Most of the producers I talked to asked which festivals I was planning to attend. It was a reasonable question, because it's a decision they make about nearly every film they produce. Would this mid-budget indie with a philosophical bent do better at Venice? Did it have the juice to aim for Cannes? Would it be ready in time for Sundance? Would a big film that's already got distribution do well by premiering at Toronto, thereby building Oscar hype before its release?

Not every producer at a festival has a movie premiering; often they're there to build buzz for a movie that's premiered elsewhere, or else secure foreign sales, reinforce connections, or discover new talent. But many of those I spoke to in the summer and fall of 2019 had been hoping to enter at least one movie at the Sundance Film Festival—the best, earliest shot of the year for an indie movie to find distribution.

"It's one of the main markets to sell a movie in the States," says Gaulding, who'd been aiming to premiere her Choctaw stickball documentary there. "Every producer shooting at a certain time has to weigh that: Are we shooting for Sundance or not?" Applicants have to send a link to the finished cut by November but *finished* is relative; Gaulding's film was uploaded multiple times to the same link as it was reedited over and over. If a movie does get accepted to Sundance, the final weeks of getting to a finished cut can be a mad, 24/7 scramble. For some, not getting in can come as a relief.

Gaulding's film didn't make the cut. The culling process is open-minded but brutal; committees composed of Sundance employees as well as people in the industry—from directors to crew members—take a first pass, then hand non-rejects over to another judge, and on and up until only a handful of pictures remain.

In late January 2020, I couldn't resist the opportunity to

see Sundance for myself, and to watch one younger producer, Kara Durrett, who actually did have a premiere.
Almost immediately on arrival, it became clear that the
producers having the most fun were the ones with no movies in the running. These unencumbered souls have come
to frigid, glitzy Park City, Utah, to spot talent, see movies,
and network. Those producers who actually have to present
a movie and sell it (God willing) seem a lot more stressed.
Take Durrett, a normally cheery woman whose patience is
being tested one late night on Park City's Main Street, as
she bickers with a bouncer outside of the after-party for her
film.

"Against the wall and back, against the wall and back,
please," the bouncer yells to the disorderly line out front, as
Durrett struggles to get crew members inside the basement
club. They take priority over herself and also a man standing politely to her side, a cinematographer who happens to
be her husband. Tomorrow she has meetings with investors
and a handful of studio executives interested in the movie
she's premiering, but tonight her job is to get her cast and
crew into her own party. "The glamorous life of the producer," she says, swallowing her exasperation.

If this kind of hassle seems counter to the spirit of independent films, it bears remembering that Sundance was always a Hollywood affair. After all, it was founded in 1978 by Robert Redford's production company. But its mission to promote indie movies reflected the iconoclastic late '60s and '70s, when filmmakers broke free of the studios to make, for example, *Butch Cassidy and the Sundance Kid*, starring Robert Redford. From the beginning, it was a showcase for indie filmmakers, producers very much included.

Today it is the largest independent film festival in the country—the prime venue for American movies that haven't yet found a distributor. But anyone who attends will tell you that it doesn't feel as independent as it used to. The ski town of Park City, beautiful and glittering in the snow, feels like a Wild West outpost gut-renovated by millionaires, which it is. The currency of the festival is the pass—or rather the right-color pass, the marker of one's influence and/or the amount of money a studio or media company is willing to spend on you. The annual showcase of movies made for accessibly low budgets trades on inaccessibility. If you don't know someone, getting a drink in Park City in the second half of January, when every storefront on Main Street is closed for a private event, is nearly impossible.

"Rejection's part of the game," says Fred Berger. "Almost

every movie I've made has been rejected by at least one festival, including the ones that have gone on to the most success."

Berger is recounting his experiences at a University of Pennsylvania alumni event for Sundance attendees, sitting on a panel with another producer and a documentary director. He's doling out advice for the casually interested as well as those passionately invested in following his path. One of his lessons: "Don't let any festival define whether your movie is good or bad."

Berger is at Sundance this year in part to support an Automatik premiere, *Run Sweetheart Run*, but he's also here to explore. Another lesson of his is that Sundance and other festivals are equally useful as an opportunity to find talent—and certainly more fun to attend in that spirit. If you're trying to sell a movie, it's a uniquely charged environment, and yet so much feels outside your control. "On one hand, it's impossible to replicate the electric energy of a festival premiere, which often leads to those storied late-night bidding wars (aka 'festival fever'). On the other hand, it's a risk; you're putting the fate of years of work in the hands of one audience and a handful of critics.

"A soft reaction in the room or a negative review can single-handedly undercut the market for your film," he continues. "Given the diminishing theatrical market for independent films, the bull's-eye for selling these films is growing narrower and scarier."

On the other hand, "Sundance is an unparalleled venue for discovery. Each year, there are remarkable new voices introduced here, which makes it an essential trip on the calendar."

Berger had just seen a short film premiering at the festival that really impressed him. "It had such confidence and precision, all on a shoestring budget. I have no doubt he'll be back here with a feature soon." For a producer, the thrill of discovery can be (almost) as big a rush as the triumph of a big, successful premiere.

There are some discoveries at the 2020 festival, as Siena Oberman reports. Without a film showing this year, she's just here to connect with people and try to see as many great movies as she can. But the overall slate is a little deflating—no amazing standouts, no truly surprising sales. *Palm Springs*, a philosophical comedy starring Andy Samberg, is the big sale of the festival. But there's something a little cynical about that, too; Hulu gets the movie for $17,500,000.69, a number clearly aimed at beating the previous Sundance sales record, for *The Birth of a Nation* in 2016, by sixty-nine cents.

"It's just a very weird year," says Oberman, after we run

into each other on Main Street. There was one movie that drove her to tears—*The Father*, starring Anthony Hopkins and Olivia Colman. But something feels off about the mood. Maybe it's the fact that the biggest celebrity this week is Hillary Clinton, whose entourage snakes its way through Main Street traffic just in time for the premiere of the documentary *Hillary*. Clinton had to settle for being feted by Hollywood, while the country had to settle for Donald Trump.

The only premiere that Automatik has is from Berger's partner Brian Kavanaugh-Jones, who has produced a feminist horror movie called *Run Sweetheart Run* with his wife, Shana Feste, the film's director and writer. Coproduced by the innovative genre producer Jason Blum, it's already set for theatrical distribution. It premieres, like other horror films, at midnight.

Since *Sweetheart* has already been sold, planning and hoping for a premiere wasn't so nerve-racking. Monique Walton, on the other hand—the Sundance Labs alum and the producer of *Bull*—had to think about Sundance and other festivals every step of the way. (Though she was affiliated with the labs, there's no leg up for alumni in getting into the festival itself.) After finding her producing partner in 2017, Walton got the movie up and running in the face of difficult logistics. The financing was touch and go and Walton had had to use her credit card. Then she had to figure out whether to aim for Sundance's 2019 festival.

"We had huge pieces that weren't shot yet, and we were trying to shoot at PBR in Austin," the Professional Bull Riders finals, which take place late in the year. "Even if we had gotten into Sundance," she says, "we would have had a real heart-to-heart about it." But their timeline prevented them from being real contenders. It was just as well; they wound up going to Cannes in May, four months later—and even that was a scramble.

One more recent fellow of the Producing Labs did have a movie at this Sundance—albeit not the film she had workshopped at the lab. Not unlike Oberman, Kara Durrett always has several films in the fire. Her lab film, *The Starling Girl*, had many complications and didn't make the festival; instead, she's here to premiere a smaller, buzzier film aiming for major distribution. Made for less than $1 million, *Save Yourselves!* features a young, hip Brooklyn couple who head for a cabin in the woods and decide to turn their phones off, thereby missing the news that aliens have taken over the world. For a sci-fi movie it's efficiently low-tech—the aliens are rat-size furballs without faces—and unusually funny. It's not *Palm Springs*, but it has the makings of a cult hit.

When I first meet Durrett at Sundance, she is standing on a packed snowbank outside the city's main library, one of many Park City buildings fitted with large auditoriums for screenings. Before heading to the greenroom to prepare for her movie's 9 p.m. premiere, she's making sure everyone who needs a ticket gets one. Needless to say, no one else involved with the movie is standing outside in the cold for forty-five minutes before it starts. Two hours later, after the first public screening of *Save Yourselves!*, she is onstage, beaming before a packed and friendly crowd. There is a Q&A, featuring the cast and heads of production.

It's a five-minute van ride to the after-party on Main Street, but it's clear the second Durrett arrives that everyone who's already gotten in wasn't at the premiere. A bouncer tells her that her own party is at capacity; no one can enter until someone leaves. It turns out that a group of hangers-on have invited friends to pack the party. Durrett isn't happy, but she can't antagonize the bouncer—and doesn't want to stress her crew, stars, or financiers.

There are dozens of people in line to get in, and they are beginning to crowd the sidewalk. "The fire department *will* shut you down if you block the street!" yells the bouncer. Durrett has no choice but to stay outside, working to get her first priorities in: the hardworking crew that literally carried the movie on their backs and the financiers she needs for this movie and her next one.

Only rarely does Durrett let her smile slide into an expression of frustration. But she relaxes when greeting friends and well-wishers, who remind her of the rapturous reception at the library. She tells me several buyers are interested, but she won't know for hours, possibly weeks, how real their interest is.

After about an hour outside, Durrett lets her husband in—and herself. The bar downstairs is maybe at 40 percent capacity. It's hard to believe that an outsize concern for fire safety is really what's behind the engineered chaos of a night out at Sundance, with at least one unruly crowd on every block from the Bridge Cafe all the way down to the Wasatch Brew Pub, obstructing the doors of temporarily branded venues like the Chase Sapphire Lounge.

Inside, gin and tonic in hand, Durrett seems to untense a little. "It's all the little details—you can't help everything that happens," she says.

"That's why she's such a special producer," says her husband. "There're a lot of producers who take the credit and do fuck-all, but she covers the entire spectrum."

"I'm not always this crazy," says Durrett. "It's usually

okay. This is crazy. Anyway, I'm gonna go say hi to financiers and try to make some money."

It will take a couple weeks for *Save Yourselves!* to find a
buyer, a non-studio distribution company called Bleecker
Street Films. It isn't nearly as big as some other distributors
that were in the mix. But after their purchase, the film is
all set for a summer 2020 opening. At its budget level, any
movie that makes it through Sundance and into theaters is
already a huge success. Like the after-party, it had a bumpy
journey, but finished strong.

By the time of the Bleecker Street purchase, mid-
February, Durrett was gearing up to debut a bigger film,
Topside, at South by Southwest. Ultimately, that didn't happen, just as *Save Yourselves!*, the comedy about the end of the
world, didn't hit theaters in the summer of 2020. Because no
films hit theaters in the summer of 2020. It was, as Oberman had observed, a very weird year.

THE FIRST CASE OF the novel coronavirus in the United
States was diagnosed a few days before Sundance opened.
Six weeks later, on March 6, South by Southwest was can-
celed, a week before its start date and just before a series

of lockdowns cascaded across the country. In addition to taking hundreds of thousands of lives in the US and millions worldwide, the COVID-19 pandemic hit every industry hard. But few were as thoroughly transformed, at least temporarily, as the business of movies and TV. By the fall of 2020 many retail establishments had reopened. But few and hardy (or foolhardy) were the souls willing to venture into movie theaters.

The quickest and most obvious casualty of this global shutdown was the summer tentpole blockbuster; movie studios relied on these to hold up the "tent" of their annual sales, and now there was nothing opening at all. The repeated postponement of Christopher Nolan's *Tenet*—until its makers finally gave up on a wide release—was just the most visible manifestation of hope giving way to despair as public-gathering prohibitions dragged on and on.

This only accelerated an existing trend in film and TV: the shift of more and more moviegoers toward watching things when and where they wanted to, which was usually on demand and at home. Platforms like Netflix and Amazon, along with new entrants like Apple TV and Disney+, stood to benefit, and so they continued to release what they had and acquire even more.

For producers it was a double life; on the one hand, they had more time and leisure to develop in-depth projects. Agencies reported that sales of book rights for adaptations were booming. Many of the initial stages of a producer's job didn't just continue; they had room to breathe. There was ample time for development and scouting; virtual networking and remote management; even some postproduction. But a producer's bread and butter (and money) comes from actual production. It's when the deals finally come through and the checks begin to clear. Barring that, producers kept busy putting many, many planes on the runway, but waiting on health officials, unions, and theater operators to clear them for takeoff.

Over those long six months, so much was lost. But something was gained, too: perspective. "At a basic level, our job is to make movies and television, and production has ground to a halt," says Berger when I check in with him in September. "It's been massively disruptive and painful. At the same time, the industry hasn't stopped moving. There has rarely been a better time to develop, package, and set up projects. We all have more bandwidth, filmmakers and actors suddenly have free time to read scripts, and buyer demand—in the midst of a content war—has only grown."

Both Berger and Oberman are back on sets for the first time in September 2020—and grateful for it. "Everyone in the industry is hungry to be shooting again, as if an essential part of us has been missing," Berger says. "It's incredibly gratifying to get those creative juices flowing again."

It's not easy, though. "All of a sudden I know so many people who are going into production," says Oberman, who is herself in the middle of prep in New York. It will be her first set since *The Birthday Cake*. Her current film, a "surreal coming-of-age drama," was supposed to start prepping back in March, the last time we'd talked. Now that it's finally happening, budgeting has become only more challenging. Between the weeks of hotel quarantine, extra staffing and testing, and especially insurance, COVID adds 20 to 25 percent to a movie's cost, and this film's budget is supposed to be under $1 million. "You can't really cut corners with safety," she says.

Studios can easily cover the costs on a sure blockbuster. A September story on COVID-era production in *The Hollywood Reporter* noted that a new *Jurassic World* production had spent $3 million on COVID testing alone. But for smaller films it's a serious burden. And that's not counting the psychological turmoil of having to police rules regarding masks, social distancing, and enforced isolation.

"It's hard to tell someone they have to sit in a hotel room for two weeks," Oberman says. "I've had reps tell me, 'My client only wants to do x number of days,' but I say it's safer to do two more days than they ask. Directors have too many things to worry about, so the producer has to worry about safety. The crew has a lot of different opinions. If they don't learn the protocols people will be kicked off set—it's happened on other productions."

In the bigger picture, this is not where Oberman had hoped to be. On her lightning-fast trajectory up through the industry, she was supposed to have moved on to bigger-budget pictures and left the smaller stuff to associates. But COVID changed those plans. *The Birthday Cake* took longer to bring to market than planned—about twenty weeks in post, which is not unusual, but that process was attenuated by the need to provide notes digitally, rather than sitting down with the editor and director in real time.

While the finished product is propulsive, occasionally funny, and ultimately shocking—and it's up for 2021 film festival consideration—the pandemic complicated the post-production process. Oberman tested the movie with focus groups, but not in real time. "Normally you can just ask people questions about what they understood and didn't, but we just did that digitally, which I think was not ideal. They just answered questions we created online. All of a sudden people become numbers instead of human beings reacting emotionally to an experience."

Oberman believes things are looking up, though she won't sugarcoat it. "Definitely a lot of people lost jobs," she says. But amid the decline of studio blockbusters, there were bright spots for independents; streaming services and VOD had largely picked up the slack, and the dearth of huge summer-swallowing films had left room in the market for smaller movies.

"There's supposed to be a lack of content coming, so hopefully indie stuff will sell well," says Oberman. "And I've heard that Toronto sales are going really well." The festivals were back, beginning in early September with the Venice Film Festival, where Berger and Oberman had premiered director Gia Coppola's film *Mainstream*—the dark social-media chronicle starring Andrew Garfield. The Toronto International Film Festival, one of the world's biggest markets, quickly followed; both were awkward, socially distanced hybrids of IRL and virtual.

In the long spring and summer of quarantine, though,

Oberman and Berger and London had had to focus on development—honing scripts, putting talent together, making pitches to distributors to get a movie off the ground.

Oberman used the production doldrums to line up several exciting projects, she says, including "an awesome female action thriller" and a true-crime thriller, "with fifth- and sixth-time directors" instead of the greener talent she's worked with to date. "I was happy that the time off allowed me to go into developing instead of worrying about production. It was actually perfect—I think it's a really good strategy to consider for the future."

She has always been in a hurry, and the 24/7 approach has gotten her far. While prepping for her September return to production, she was back to working past midnight every night. But the earlier break had forced her to think a little more strategically—not just about her movies but about the future of the production company, Artemis. She has turned down several offers from financiers to back the company, mostly out of concern for her creative freedom. Now she's decided she'd rather wait and get some bigger projects off the ground—define her brand more selectively and purposefully—before entertaining any potential partners.

Oberman's ultimate goal is not to do more but actually

less—one or two bigger indie movies a year instead of five smaller ones. Berger, too, plans to scale back on the volume of projects even as the budgets scale up. Helping Berger and Automatik with that mission is a deal the company sealed just as everything began to close down in March— a comprehensive first-look deal with Amazon. In effect, they are on the studio lot—though the studio is virtual and streaming.

Berger is quick to recognize that the human losses of the pandemic have been devastating in every sense. For his projects, the results have so far been mixed. The choose-your-own-adventure streaming series he was staffing up in the late fall of 2019 in New York still hasn't filmed yet but is set for a summer 2021 shoot. The high-profile biopic has to find a new production date with shifting talent schedules. Brian Kavanaugh-Jones's *Run Sweetheart Run* had shelved its theatrical opening and gone with Amazon as a streamer instead. But projects in earlier phases are coming along. The musical film about the underdog, the subject of Berger's early-morning pitch, is moving forward, having found development financing, and the sci-fi movie on which he'd taken the belt-tightening budget pass has found a home and a green light; those SUVs might just be helicopters again.

Michael London, with his slate of projects mostly in development, has endured the shutdown of production a little less directly but no less acutely. "We're under stress, like every company," he says. "Without shows moving to production, buyers have been a lot more cautious about moving things through the pipeline. That's been a battle, but we've also been really productive and managed to get some high-profile new projects sold."

Snowfall's fourth season will soon come out of an unexpected COVID hiatus. As for development, London has managed to roll some of his boulders close to the hilltop, while others have gathered moss—fairly typical of his long road to success.

Yellow Bird has gotten a little more complicated but mostly for the better. Sterlin Harjo had a pilot at FX greenlit, and so, now that he was busier, Groundswell brought in a cowriter whom Harjo was close to—Erica Tremblay. "She's been a wonderful addition to the team," says London, "because as a Native woman she has had a lot of experiences that related to Lissa's story." It's especially important to have that female presence because Susannah Grant, the writer London had been courting, wound up being unavailable after all.

The good news is that Beau Willimon, the creator and showrunner of *House of Cards*, has come on board as a creative overseer of the project. They're all working on "cracking the pilot" and honing a pitch, confident that Willimon's track record will help them secure a big commitment from a major platform.

Other projects have shifted serendipitously, too. After the famous playwright had stepped aside from working on the literary classic, the same agent suggested another writer, an English showrunner with a long list of successful credits. London had begun conversations with him and within weeks, they agreed on a fresh creative approach. A big new commercial platform had swooped in and bought the project, hoping to add a little literary prestige to their growing slate.

Meanwhile, the director who asked for a bigger budget on the multigenerational book adaptation has moved on, and now London is working with a new director who is approaching the movie on a more modest scale. The Taj Mahal project was, temporarily, a COVID casualty—picked up by a financier and then dropped when the pandemic forced them to back out of new commitments. But the extra time allowed them to reimagine a new version, based on *Empress*, a book by Ruby Lal about Nur Jahan, a uniquely power-ful woman in the Mughal Empire—making for a proto-feminist story that's "much more relevant and timely" and not coincidentally a hotter prospect. In other words, all that weekend reading seems to be paying off months down the line.

There's been more weekend reading in general, given the slower pace. London says he has felt some relief in being able to develop projects more intensively, with an eye on the bigger picture. But he's ready to move on—itchy as the oth-ers to get into production. "After six months of it, the nov-elty of having time to think and relax wears off, and it starts to become frustrating that there's so much uncertainty in the business."

The financial stress is concerning, but London can af-ford to take a broader view. "People have been stuck in their homes where they are watching programming and want to consume television shows and movies," he says. "Ultimately there will be a really healthy rebound, predicated on things getting back into production. The fact that less of it will be in movie theaters, that's just the new reality of Hollywood."

London had already adapted just fine to the shift away from theaters even before 2020. In fact, he's been through all of it already: the comfort of the studio job, the adrenaline rush of scrappy indie survival, the largesse of the financiers and then the 2008 crash, followed by the rise of TV. He's been able to adapt before, and he almost relishes the prospect of doing so again.

Oberman and Berger, meanwhile—producers a little more accustomed to working at breakneck speed—are starting to realize that downtime has its benefits. Even after COVID subsides, they are looking to work productive sabbaticals into their careers at strategic moments.

"Nothing can justify the far-reaching tragedies of this year, which have disproportionately impacted underprivileged communities," says Berger. "We don't take for granted that our work can largely continue seamlessly from home. If anything, we've all learned how much time we were wasting driving across town for pitches and meetings that can happen as effectively over Zoom. It's been a useful moment for reset and self-reflection and invaluable time with our families. We're constantly running—from one set to another, treading water to stay afloat. We've rarely had time to reflect on our priorities."

Berger spent the summer rewatching the classics of the '90s—and the '70s, too—relearning some aesthetic lessons and supplementing "output" with input. He's been watching contemporary shows, too, and thought a lot about one in particular: *The Last Dance*, the summer's Netflix documentary series about Michael Jordan and the Chicago Bulls.

"Jordan was a dominant player from the day he entered the league," says Berger, "but what allowed him to *win* was the off-season, coming off of crushing losses. He would learn to play within a team framework or physically reshape his body. The pivotal work was done during those summers. Without those breaks, who knows if he would have won six championships. Again, let's be clear, the devastating costs of this pandemic far outweigh the silver linings, but in terms of having this period to retrain, refocus, recharge—I think we'll emerge stronger."

It shouldn't be too surprising that these producers have found a way to learn and improve even in a time of unfathomable crisis. They're wired for persistence, for adaptation. Like the ever-changing industry itself, every project of theirs is a moving target; no two are alike, nor do they demand exactly the same set of skills. The most important thing you learn from watching masterful producers at work is that they are not aiming to make the perfect movie or show. They want to make the best version of the project they're working on. And then, if it doesn't work out that particular time, usually for reasons beyond their control, they are convinced there's another opportunity just ahead. If you want to be a producer, there really is no alternative to thinking that way, in good and bad times. Succeeding in the long term means knowing how to win *and* lose and then win again. There's no other way to play the game.

ACKNOWLEDGMENTS

Producers love publicity for their finished projects, but they tend to avoid it for themselves and their delicate works in progress. Those who spoke to me all overcame this natural reticence out of a belief that it would help dispel some myths and provide the kind of primer on producing that they didn't have in their youth. I'm deeply grateful for their generosity, guidance, and trust. Chief among them are Fred Berger, Siena Oberman, and Michael London, who shared their professional lives with me. Thanks go to their colleagues as well: Shannon Gaulding, Jordan Mahoney, and Sarah Freedman at Groundswell; Brian Kavanaugh-Jones and the entire team at Grandview/Automatik; Jimmy Giannopoulos, Raul Bermudez, and the rest of the cast and crew of *The Birthday Cake*. Thank you to Lynda Obst and Anne Lai for their time and wisdom, Kara Durrett and Monique Walton for their honesty and idealism. Other people—they know who they are—helped forge the connections and provide the context without which none of this would have been possible. My editor, Stuart Roberts, along with the Simon & Schuster team—including Emily Simonson,

Christine Calella, Dominick Montalto, and Jonathan Evans—were skilled and caring and (crucially) boundlessly patient. Jofie Ferrari-Adler guided me toward "Masters at Work" and edited my first two books. Thanks to Jofie for everything; one day soon we'll be together again. Thank you to Julia Turner at the *Los Angeles Times* for giving me the space and time to finish this project (and for much else besides, including a new life). And all my love to Jamie and Asher—always, but in this case for tolerating those late nights at the laptop, those early trips to L.A., and finally the big move to that new life.

APPENDIX: FIND OUT MORE

There's been no shortage of films, books, shows or publications that mystify and glamorize Hollywood, but precious few that explain how it works. That's begun to change, especially as the industry itself becomes more open to outsiders. Here are some good (and entertaining) sources to help you get started.

BOOKS

Easy Riders, Raging Bulls by Peter Biskind (Simon & Schuster, 1999)
Down and Dirty Pictures by Peter Biskind (Simon & Schuster, 2004)

Biskind's two books together encompass the two great waves of independent filmmaking, and while both are rich in industry gossip—never stinting on affairs, drugs, and other assorted misbehavior—both give the full context on changes in the industry that allowed the masterpieces of the '70s and the '90s to flourish. *Easy Riders* begins with that moment in the late '60s when the studio system began to break apart and bold new voices filled the vacuum—Scorsese, Coppola, Redford, De Niro, et al. *Down and Dirty Pictures* documents the rise of Miramax, Redford's Sundance Film Festival, and all of Fred Berger's favorite filmmakers, again paying attention to the production and business side while giving the outsize personalities plenty of room to breathe (and yell).

Shooting to Kill by Christine Vachon (William Morrow, 1998)

The cofounder of Killer Films has worked on a smaller scale than Miramax—which actually makes her more prototypical of the DIY independent producer. Working the edgiest corners of the '90s boom (*Kids, Happiness, Boys Don't Cry*), Vachon built up not just experience but broad expertise. Part memoir and part how-to, Vachon's manual on small-budget filmmaking even includes a fully detailed line-item production budget. If you really want to know how it's done and the kind of nerve it takes to do it, dive in.

Hello, He Lied by Lynda Obst (Crown, 1997)

Obst provided valuable insights for this book, but they're the tip of the iceberg. Her first memoir of her time in the industry, on producing movies ranging from *Sleepless in Seattle* to *The Fisher King*, offers much more. Obst walks you through every step of the process in amusing detail and has a gift for aphorisms. She breaks down both the tactics and the strategy of doing the job well—everything from setting the right budgetary expectations to managing romantic relationships with colleagues.

The Complete Film Production Handbook, Fourth Edition by Eve Light Honthaner (Focal Press, 2010)

Memoirs are fun, but anyone looking to know the soup-to-nuts details of every phase of the production process—from the rules governing various unions to the release forms and contracts every producer uses—will find it all here. It's an essential textbook of the industry, whether or not you go to film school.

PODCASTS

The Producer's Guide

Host Todd Garner is a prolific producer (everything from *Paul Blart* to the *xXx* franchise), and his show brings a producer's-eye view to all his interviews and audio essays, even as his guests range widely: WWE's John Cena; director Eli Roth; Jeremy Zinner, CEO of the agency UTA.

Life With Caca

This show from producer Carolina "Caca" Groppa is one of the precious few devoted to what it's like to be a film producer in the trenches. From Eva Longoria to the producer of *It*, guests on the show get into just enough of the fine-print nitty-gritty to fill in the texture of the job, but they spend just as much time on the emotional ups and downs of working today, in a time of COVID and growing calls for diversity.

Scriptnotes

While technically a show about screenwriting, this industry favorite runs the gamut of Hollywood production. Hosted by writer Craig Mazin, creator of *Chernobyl*, and Jack-of-most trades John August (*Charlie's Angels*, *Big Fish*, *Aladdin*), this podcast hits recurring segments like "Deep Dive" and "How Would This Be a Movie" that interrogate the process of assimilating artistic visions into the Hollywood machine.

Indie Film Hustle

Independent filmmaker Alex Ferrera has had a long career as a kind of gonzo journeyman, never being precious about the jobs he takes. He brings the same freewheeling spirit to this top-rated show, focused on tricks of the trade and such topical issues as COVID-related film piracy and lessons the low-budget filmmaker can learn from *The Mandalorian*.

MAGAZINES AND WEBSITES

The Trades

Recall that David Permut, at age thirteen, learned the trade by reading *Variety*. A sure way to gauge your interest in the industry process—a sort of gateway drug into the professional life—is picking up one of the trade papers that proliferated since Permut's youth in the '60s. The classic *Variety* now competes with *The Hollywood Reporter*, *Deadline*, and a handful of smaller publications. Among those, *IndieWire* is not just top-notch but also the most indie-oriented and the handiest for readers who haven't yet made all the connections they'll need.

Filmmaker magazine

A print quarterly that's really the front for an incredibly robust website, *Filmmaker* combines the gloss of a snappy trade publication with smartly packaged how-to essays. Columns by insiders who happen to be fine writers (including producers) gives a sense of the life from many perspectives, while a "Filmmaking" vertical subdivided by career tracks (including producing) offers specific tips and in-depth interviews up and down the production line.

FilmSchool.org

It's not all about USC and UCLA. This site is a one-stop shop for anyone considering the academic route, offering reviews of various institutions, news and features, community forums and clubs, and an "Application Tracker" linking to applications forms for entry to more than 2,700 institutions.